Polish Wedding Customs & Traditions

Also by Sophie Hodorowicz Knab:

Polish Customs, Traditions and Folklore

Polish Herbs, Flowers and Folk Medicine

Polish Wedding Customs & Traditions

Sophie Hodorowicz Knab

HIPPOCRENE BOOKS
New York

For information, address:
HIPPOCRENE BOOKS, INC.
171 Madison Avenue
New York, NY 10016

Library of Congress Cataloging-in-Publication Data

Knab, Sophie Hodorowicz.
Polish wedding customs & traditions / Sophie Knab.
p. cm.
Includes bibliographical references and index.
ISBN 0-7818-0530-9
1. Wedding etiquette—Poland. 2. Weddings-Planning. 3. Marriage
Customs and rites—Poland. I. Title.
BJ2051.LK53 1997
392.5'089'9185—dc21   97-26010
                                                 CIP
                                                  AC

Printed in the United States of America

Dedicated to my nieces...

Catherine Hodorowicz
Mary Theresa Hodorowicz
Amy Hodorowicz

May you always be proud of your Polish heritage.

ACKNOWLEDGMENTS

I am deeply grateful to the following individuals:

Mark Kohan, editor-in-chief of the *Polish American Journal* and a great Polish-American musician, for his enthusiastic assistance and the numerous discussions we had about wedding music;

Rev. Czesław Krysa, Mrs. Sophie Krysa, Henia and Joe Makowski, Frank and Judy Krauza, Estelle Kasprzyk, Lorraine Keifer, Annette Junciewicz Olma, Frank and Jadzia Dziegielewski, Jessie Miecznikowski, Barbara Frackiewicz, Brian Stanish and Emily Stanish, Maria and Tadeusz Pyzikiewicz, and Michael Drabik for their constant emotional support and encouragement, for help in translating arcane Polish words, lending books, photographs and articles, and sharing memories.

The librarians and staff at Niagara County Community College who give unstintingly of their time, energy and resources to make my books possible.

Mark Mistriner of the Culinary Arts Department at Niagara County Community College for reviewing the wedding menus and offering some good suggestions; Krystyna Bartosik at the Warsaw Ethnographic Museum for her constant willingness to send books, articles and photographs.

Hippocrene Books, Inc., for their continued commitment to publish books of interest to the Polish American community.

To all of you, *Bóg zapłac*.

CONTENTS

Introduction

*I*f you picked up this book, you are probably looking for a way to reflect the importance of your Polish heritage on one of the most important days of your life. It is my hope that this book will help you do just that.

Every bride wants her wedding day to stand out as special among all the other days of her life. She wants it to be a day she will remember forever with great happiness and a sense of deep satisfaction. As a result, a lot of time and energy is devoted to reading the latest bridal magazines, attending numerous fashion shows, examining color swatches, looking at various reception sites and talking with caterers, florists, and band leaders. She also wants it to be special and unique—a perfect day filled with warmth, love and laughter. She wants the day to have that certain something that would truly distinguish her wedding from others. Today, more and more people are taking a new interest and pride in the traditions of their forefathers by incorporating them into their everyday lives, as well as on special occasions. This book is about making your wedding a very personal statement—a reflection of who you are, what you believe in, and what you value.

Polish weddings of the past include many of the same rites and rituals that are known throughout the rest of the world. There were, however, some customs that were unique to Poland. Among these are the very moving and heartfelt blessing ceremony, the greeting of guests with bread and salt, and the unique *oczepiny* (capping) ceremony, the special rite-of-passage when the bride is symbolically transformed from a single woman to a married one. Each of these unique customs are explained as thoroughly as possible so as to be understandable and easily implemented. I have also gone to great pains to find information about clothes, jewelry, and traditional flowers because these, too, are an important part of Polish wedding history and can add those special touches to a wedding that lift it above the ordinary. Priscilla of Boston, the famous bridal gown designer, has been quoted as saying that she prefers the ethnic wedding to the "boring, uptight society affair" even if it does mean extra work for her to design a special gown that could withstand the rigors of ethnic weddings.

As you read this book, choose the customs that have meaning for you or feel right for you and omit those that don't. Customs from the past are not intended to be used in a very rigid manner. Instead, they can serve as a source of ideas to create a wedding that is special and meaningful. Don't shy away from celebrating your heritage at your wedding because you don't feel comfortable doing everything that is traditional. Combine diverse elements that represent who you are and where you have come from. Poland's acceptance of Christianity in 966 resulted in Catholic rites and rituals being tightly woven into all aspects of personal and public life, including the customs and traditions associated with weddings. This, however, is no reason why you should not have the wedding of which you have always dreamed. Over the centuries Polish women have been married in palaces, cathedrals, wooden churches, roadside chapels and in the parlors of their own homes. They've exchanged their marriage vows during the day, in the evening and even in secret in the dead of night. There have been arranged marriages, runaway marriages, trick marriages, marriage by proxy, abductions and, last but not least, marriages based on love and mutual regard. Everything was not always conducted in the standard, traditional manner. There was a lot of spontaneity and improvisation. So trust your feelings and instincts. If you desire to marry in a garden or aboard a yacht instead of in church, do so. If it is an interfaith marriage, have it co-officiated if that's what appeals to you and your groom. Register with a gift registry and toss the bridal bouquet. There is no right way or wrong way to plan a wedding. All that is important is that it reflects the way the bride and groom want to celebrate this very important day.

There are few things that can make a wedding more unique than drawing upon the past and reviving ancient and long forgotten customs and traditions. These traditions have the power to transform what would be a nice wedding into a truly unforgettable one, rich with substance and meaning. Anyone who has ever attended a traditional Italian, Greek, Irish or Mexican wedding will tell you that the joy and communal spirit that is present at these affairs is truly unmatched among social occasions.

Chapter I

The Engagement

To be the moon dust at your feet,
the wind through your ribbon, the milk in your cup
the cigarette in your lips, the path among the cornflowers
you walk through, the bench on which your rest, the book
        you read.
To be sewn into you like thread, to surround you like space,
to be the seasons for your dear eyes to see,
and the fire in your chimney, and the roof which protects you
        from the rain.

        "Moon Dust"
        —Konstanty Ildefons Gałczyński (1905-1953)

The Hope Chest

There was once a time when getting married had little to do with romance. The union of a man and a woman was more of a business deal than a matter of the heart, and was used as a means of uniting empires and fortunes. Whether she possessed a tremendous fortune or a small one, a young woman was expected to bring something valuable to the marriage. The wealth that the bride brought her groom on their marriage day was called a dowry. It consisted of money, jewelry, a deed to a piece of property or other tangible items such as livestock. This was so critically important that a poor young woman without a thing to bring to a marriage was often overlooked in favor of someone else. One of Poland's more important feast

11

Dowry chest painted with flowers, c. 18-19th century.

days, the Feast of St. Nicholas on December 6, celebrates among other things, the life of a man who helped three young women receive a dowry.

According to legend, an impoverished nobleman had three daughters who remained unmarried because he could not provide them with dowries. Upon hearing this, St. Nicholas took gold pieces from his coffers and on the night of December 5, threw them into the window of the house. With this dowry, the eldest daughter was able to wed a man of noble birth. St. Nicholas did this again for the other two daughters so that they, too, could marry. This legend was the basis for the establishment of a special fund called the coffer of St. Nicholas. It was founded by a very wealthy woman in Cracow in the sixteenth century. She designated a large sum of money for poor girls who wished to marry. Over the next several centuries this foundation prospered and whatever candidates were chosen to receive funds did so on the Feast Day of St. Nicholas, in honor of the man who first made the dowries possible. This dowry fund continued until 1932.

A young man contemplating marriage often sought to improve his social and financial status by choosing a bride with some type of dowry. The prospective bride was also often expected to bring clothes for herself and items for the establishment of a home. As a result, it wasn't unusual for an ambitious mother, who wished to see her daughter marry well, to begin plotting, planning and collecting the items that her daughter could offer a prospective groom. By the time a young girl began budding into woman-hood and understood the necessity for these items, she, too, began planning and preparing. The items were placed into a special trunk or wedding chest called a dowry chest, which later came to be known as a "hope" chest.

The oldest type of dowry or "hope" chests in Poland date back as early as the fifteenth century, but they really became prominent in the seventeenth and eighteenth centuries. The most beautiful dowry chests were the painted chests. Among the items listed in a last will and testament in 1684 were "two large chests, one black and one yellow, each with painted flowers." In another last will and testament, dated 1764, "a green chest with flowers" was listed among the pieces of furniture.

The typical painted chest was made of pine and was rectangular in shape. The top lid was flat and often had a lock and key. Because it was very large, it sometimes stood on wheels to facilitate movement. The chests were handsomely dovetailed and sometimes had drawers at the bottom. Some had special compartments inside for holding papers and money.

The chests were made by local joiners and carpenters or by a skilled individual who knew how to work with wood and made furniture during the long winter months for extra money. What made the chest special was the decorations painted on the front, sides and top of the chest. These were created by itinerant artists painting freehand or by the carpenters themselves, with the help of stencils. First, the entire chest was painted. Many regions of Poland had their own preferred color for the background color including yellow, green, red and blue. On this background color, the artists painted flowerpots or vases filled with tulips or roses. Sometimes the artist chose to paint a bouquet of flowers such as daisies or carnations tied with a ribbon. Birds with brightly colored plumage were also a common motif. If someone custom-ordered a chest, the owner often had the year painted on or their name or initials. These painted chests, sold locally at the fairs and marketplaces, were very desirable items. Marriageable young girls and their mothers often saved their egg and butter money for years and observed the strictest of economies in their housekeeping in order to be able to afford a painted chest as part of a dowry.

By the nineteenth century, the popularity of the painted chests began to wane. They were replaced by the more "modern" and fashionable chests of the unpainted variety. These were very sturdy and functional chests made of oak, poplar or beech. Their decoration was not with paint but in the hardware. Blacksmiths made very decorative iron handles, locks and hinges as well as elaborate hardware simply for adornment on the front, top and sides of the chest. The year of purchase or the initials of the owner were sometimes cut into the hardware.

The dowry chest, whether a brightly painted one or a simple plain one, with or without fancy hardware, was considered to be one of the most important pieces of furniture in a country cottage. In most regions of Poland the chest was placed against a wall in the main room, perhaps under a window where a housewife could sit and do a bit of mending by the light. In the north of Poland, where four-poster canopied beds were common, the chest was placed at the foot of the bed.

The chest was eventually replaced by wardrobes and chests of drawers which became common in the nineteenth century, but before that time, the dower chest served many purposes. In homes where space was minimal, the chest also served as an extra place to sit and even sleep. It was a storage place for important papers such as deeds to property, marriage certificates and money. Sunday-best clothes were also stored here, away from moths and insects. Linen sheets and pillowcases, dried in the open air on a clothesline on a sunny day, were carefully folded between sprigs of lavender and stored in the chest until needed.

Another important item necessary for a newly married couple was a bed. Every young woman embarking on marriage struggled to have all the necessary items for her marriage bed. A comforter made of feathers and down was (and still is) called a *pierzyna* in Poland. This was considered an essential item for any girl entering marriage. In preparation for this, the housewife began raising geese and saving the feathers to make each daughter a thick pierzyna. Long winter nights were spent stripping feathers off the quill. The soft feathers were stored in bags in the attic until enough had been accumulated over the years to make a down comforter and pillows.

The comforter generally consisted of goose down or a mixture of down with other feathers stuffed into a very tightly woven fabric so that the feathers would not poke through. This was then slipped into another covering made of a finer linen cloth and held in place by a row of buttons along the top. The thicker and higher the comforter, the better. Along with feather pillows, the comforter was an indicator of some means, if not actual wealth.

Other items that were kept in the chest were sheets and pillowcases. In the past, most sheets and pillowcases were made at home. Polish women harvested their own flax plants and spun the long, silky fibers of the plant into different grades of thread. The housewife and her daughter generally took pains to spin a very fine thread, knowing that the finer the thread, the smoother and softer the fabric. This fine linen thread was destined to be woven into lengths of fabric, either at home on the family loom or taken to a local weaver. The bolts of finished linen fabric were then cut and sewn into sheets and pillowcases. Oftentimes, the young woman embroidered designs on the pillowcases using threads dyed with indigo or using natural dyes from plants found in the fields. If possible, a fine linen tablecloth was woven to cover the table for special holidays, especially the *Wigilia*, or Christmas Eve supper, or for the Easter breakfast, called *Święconka*. The second grade of spun thread was thicker and coarser. This sturdier thread was woven into cloth that would be used for rougher work, such as dish towels or sacking to store herbs and mushrooms.

Later, when cheap production of cotton made it a more affordable choice for everyday domestic products, cotton became the fabric of choice in many Polish homes. Bolts of cotton cloth were made into pillowcases that were then embroidered or embellished with hand-crocheted edgings. Sometimes a cotton-linen combination was used to weave into cloth.

White-on-white embroidery, which developed during the Renaissance, was especially popular in the mountain regions of Poland. In the nineteenth century, it was customary in these mountain cottages to embroider pillowcases and to edge sheets with embroidery and lace. When bedspreads became the mode, women used white embroidered sheets over their pillows and comforters. White eyelet curtains were also made for the windows. Doilies were embroidered for small tables and shelves.

Lace, also invented during the Renaissance, was so expensive that it was considered a form a wealth, in the same league as precious stones and money. Bobbin lace originated in Flanders and needle lace in Venice. Both were quickly copied and adopted all over Europe, including Poland. The rich ordered sumptuous bed and table linens from expert needleworkers for their residences and palaces. Lacemaking became an accomplishment of well-born females, many of whom learned the art in convent schools. Female servants learned the finer arts from their mistresses simply through observation and copying. Lacemaking soon became a cottage industry. Then, in the mid-nineteenth century, factory lacemaking looms redefined the lace industry, making traditionally handcrafted items available at an affordable price for all classes of people. Even those living in humble cottages tried to enhance the look of their homes with small amounts of lace on linens and bedding.

The very wealthy were concerned about having appropriate amounts of linens and lace in the dowry. In noble and royal families, the dowry brought by a bride was generally seen as a stepping stone towards building power and wealth and often determined policies of state. Bona Sforza, the Italian princess who became the wife of King Zygmunt I (1467-1548) of Poland, did not neglect to bring an appropriate amount of bed linen to her marriage. All of the twenty sheets she took to Poland as part of her dowry were embroidered with lilies, roses and leaves in colored silk threads.

Among the many items Bona brought with her were all the necessary bedroom furnishings. The main item was an enormous bed made from carved and gilded wood; four mattresses covered with blue silk and embroidered with silver and silk threads; pillows; and a coverlet sewn with gold braiding. The four-poster bed had a black velvet and white satin canopy and was trimmed with gold braid. There were twenty-three different sets of bed curtains, which were exceptionally elegant, and eighteen other coverlets for the bed. Twelve were made of brocade, six from tafetta and the rest made of silk with embroidery in a Turkish motif. To lay in front of the bed, Bona brought two small rugs.

The soon-to-be Polish queen also brought clothes and sleepwear. Amidst the one hundred and fifteen shirts were twelve nightshirts made from Holland cloth and embroidered on the sleeves and around the neck. Two nightshirts, designated for her new husband, were made of gold cloth and exquisitely embroidered. Seventeen other shirts were made with fabric from Flanders with bands of gold. Twelve robes with gold bands and wide sleeves were also for her husband. She also brought with her one hundred and twenty handkerchiefs, hemmed with gold or colored silk threads, of which thirty-six were for the king.

Bona Sforza also thought ahead to the time when she would be dining and entertaining visiting dignitaries. She brought to her marriage a table loaded with silver, two pitchers with matching bowls, six large cups, twelve platters, twelve flat plates and twenty-four deep ones, a salt cellar, a box to hold table napkins, knives and forks, four large candlesticks, two carboys and a pail—all made of silver. A gold goblet was to be a present for her husband. To fill the sideboard that she was also bringing to the marriage, there were sixty-four tablecloths. Besides bringing forty-eight reels of leather to cover the walls of the castle, Flemish tapestries and portraits of her ancestors, she brought several personal items for herself such as bottles for cosmetics and perfumes made from gold and silver, beautifully framed mirrors, and an abundance of jewelry.

Another source of information about the dowries of Polish women of the past comes to us from diaries. There were Polish women at the turn of the century who kept a running account of their lives through diaries. In doing so, they unwittingly managed to document the essence of day-to-day living in addition to the important occasions and holidays of those times. One of these was a well-to-do woman named Marianna

Malinowska Jasiecki who began keeping a journal of her life in the year 1892 on the suggestion of her sister. In it we learn not only about common everyday events, worries and tribulations, but also of the weddings of her daughters. A long excerpt from that diary, found towards the end of this book, contains interesting and revealing comments about the wedding and all the wedding preparations. What is of interest at this point are the comments regarding the dowry and household items that her daughter received for her wedding. Marianna writes: "I glue to my diary a separate list of the wedding trousseau of my daughter, Rose, beginning with the cost and then itemizing the table cutlery, china, linens for the table, bedding and personal linen. I have truly tired myself out counting and writing out these items but this will serve me in the future when I will be preparing the trousseaus of my younger daughters. One must not lament the work involved... Rosie's dowry is to be in the form of cash which Michael will pay at the time of the signing of the marriage and it will be secured by notary to Boguliński (groom) in Środa."

The list attached to Marianna's diary itemizes all that her daughter, Rose, took with her to start her new household.

Dowry of Rose Jaciecka Bogulińska, married December 29, 1900

Table Linen

1 linen tablecloth that sits twelve with twelve matching napkins in a flowered cyclamen design
1 linen tablecloth for six with five napkins in a flowered cyclamen design
1 linen tablecloth for eight in flowered rose pattern
1 linen tablecloth for six with six napkins in a flowered design
1 damask tablecloth that will sit twenty-four individuals with twenty-four matching damask napkins
1 damask tablecloth without napkins in a rose design
2 linen tablecloths (c.1815) from great-grandmother Petronella Malinowska
10 tablecloths for everyday use and thirty-six napkins for everyday use

Table Linens for Serving Coffee

1 rose colored linen tablecloth and twelve napkins
1 yellow linen tablecloth and six napkins

1 beige tablecloth with hand embroidered roses and eight matching napkins
1 stripped tablecloth with red cross stitching and eight napkins
12 napkins embroidered with fruit
6 napkins with colored embroidery
6 variously embroidered napkins for small tables
1 white silk tablecloth for the parlor
1 pale blue silk tablecloth
2 tablecloths that sit twelve individuals, one with a frieze border and the other in rose
1 tablecloth for eight in a trellis pattern with roses and a black border
2 yellow tablecloths that will accommodate six individuals
1 homespun tablecloth with red and blue embroidery
2 tablecloths for the parlor in Richelieu embroidery

Blankets and Bedding

10 pillows
4 pierzynas (down comforters)
4 mattress covers
2 light red satin coverlets
2 dark red satin coverlets
2 rose colored silk coverlets
2 crimson silk coverlets
2 plush bedspreads
2 rugs for near the bed
2 rugs for the guest rooms
4 green silk coverlets for the guest rooms
2 blue satin coverlets for the guest rooms
1 beige coverlet embroidered in red flowers
2 plush bedspreads for the guest rooms
2 pillows for the sofa
1 paisley shawl
3 decorative guest towels embroidered in the Kaszuby style with bouquets of roses and grapes
2 large sheets for the guest room

Bed Linen

4 duvets of white linen for the pierzynas (down comforters)
4 duvets made of cotton
2 batiste duvets

2 duvets for the coverlets with panels of Swiss embroidery
2 duvets for the coverlets in embroidered batiste
4 duvets for the coverlets without inserts
2 duvets in stripes
4 everyday duvets
12 linen sheets
12 batiste sheets
12 everyday sheets
2 linen pillowcases with embroidered flounces
2 batiste pillowcases with embroidered flounces
4 pillowcases with pleats
4 pillowcases without pleats
4 linen pillowcases with lace
4 pillowcases with tulle
4 pillowcases with everyday embroidery
4 pillowcases with embroidery at the corners
4 pillowcases with white embroidery
8 smooth batiste pillows

Towels

1 dozen white linen towels
1 dozen white linen towels in a flower design
1 dozen white linen towels with a swan design
1 dozen smaller white linen towels
4 bath towels
6 large bath towels
6 hand embroidered towels
1 dozen kitchen towels with blue and white stripes
1 dozen kitchen towels with gray and white stripes
13 larger linen dish towels
12 smaller linen dish towels
12 smaller towels for dusting
3 linen mangling cloths
4 linen covers for the ironing board

The list of linens is impressive even by today's standards, but was customary for the times. Items were bought to last for decades and even a lifetime. Marianna reminds us of this when she writes: "the bed and table linens should last into the next generation and if the family fails to increase and the house doesn't grow any larger, then her entire trousseau should certainly last her a lifetime." The rest of her trousseau included:

Silver cutlery pieces

1 complete set of 18 pieces of silverware including dinner knives, forks, soup, dessert, tea and coffee spoons
6 silver dinner knives
6 silver dessert knives
2 silver ladles
2 serving spoons
2 serving forks

Everyday silver cutlery

1 complete set of 18 pieces of silverware with spoons, knives and forks in a sheaf pattern
18 little spoons for coffee in sheaf pattern
2 silver napkin rings
2 plates for serving cake and fruit
1 soup ladle
1 serving spoon and fork
1 spoon and fork for serving salads
1 sugar spoon
1 spoon for tortes

Glassware

18 cut crystal glasses for tea
18 cut crystal glasses for beer
18 large cut crystal wine goblets
18 smaller cut crystal red wine goblets
12 crystal goblets for Rhenish wine
18 crystal plates for cake
2 crystal cake plates
18 knife and fork rests
2 crystal salt shakers
2 cut crystal water carafes
2 cut crystal juice carafes
6 goblets for water
4 cut crystal carafes for vodka
18 cut crystal vodka glasses
1 crystal teapot

Personal clothing

12 linen blouses with hand embroidery on the front
6 linen blouses with gussets
2 batiste blouses with lace and embroidery
6 plain linen blouses
6 batiste blouses with drawnwork
6 batiste nightgowns
12 batiste night jackets
12 warmer night jackets
3 batiste dressing gowns for hair dressing
4 short night jackets
6 white summer skirts
4 white lighterweight summer skirts
4 white heavierweight skirts
12 pairs of batiste bloomers with embroidery
12 pairs of batiste bloomers without embroidery
12 pairs of linen bloomers
1 warm rose colored morning jacket
1 warm blue morning jacket
1 dressy wool rose colored morning jacket
1 dressy blue morning jacket
3 lightweight colored morning jackets
4 scarves
96 handkerchiefs for the nose: muslin, batiste, for visiting and for balls
8 white embroidered aprons
10 colored aprons
1 dozen thin stockings
1 dozen medium-weight stockings
1 dozen warm stockings
6 lightweight camisoles
6 heavier-weight camisoles
6 beautiful slips
2 beautiful silk slips
1 slip for ballgowns

Ideas to borrow from the past:

- If your engagement is going to be a long one, begin collecting items
  in a traditional "hope" chest. There are still numerous stores that sell
  beautiful chests of all kinds. Very old painted chests can still be found

in better antique shops but because of their age can be very expensive. Reproduction painted chests are available at better furniture stores at costs that are more manageable.

- Ask for a traditional linen shower—sheets, pillowcases, blankets, down pillows and a down comforter to help create a bedroom filled with comfort, romance and history. Also appropriate would be fine tablecloths for special entertaining, dish towels, bath towels, etc.

Traditional Times for Engagements

Today engagements and weddings occur almost any day and any time of the year. In old Poland most engagements and weddings took place from September until the end of November. There were very practical reasons for this. Both spring and summer were seasons devoted to the critically important tasks of crop planting and harvesting. These jobs consumed every minute of the day and left little leisure time for merriment and festivities. Among both the rich and the poor, the end of the summer season meant that the harvest had been successfully brought in, and there was enough food and money to host a major celebratory event such as a wedding. Wintertime, right after Christmas, and very early spring, were also traditional seasons for weddings. The exceptions were Lent and Advent. Because of strict adherences to these solemn periods on the Catholic calendar, weddings were never held during these times.

Ideas to borrow from the past:

- The traditional wedding time of winter makes for a perfect Christmas wedding. Dressed in luxurious white velvet, rich brocades of deep green, ruby red, or cream satin will echo Polish weddings of the past, especially if the ceremony takes place in a massive cathedral. Church decorations of dark evergreens, ivy, misletoe, boxwood, and deep red roses can make for a stunning wedding celebration.

The Engagement

In small towns and rural villages, there was generally a very short engagement period that lasted three weeks—the time it took to read the banns in the church. Among the wealthier classes, where marriages of convenience were arranged to align powerful families and fortunes, engagements often lasted much longer. Not only were there elaborate preparations to begin, and pre-nuptial agreements to contract, but guests were often invited from other parts of Poland and Europe. Days and weeks were required for traveling the distance to the wedding and, once arrived, these guests often stayed on for weeks and months after the wedding to visit with their hosts and nearby neighbors. All this required a great deal of planning and organization on the part of the hosting families.

In today's time, the announcement of an engagement often comes as no surprise to either family or friends. Very often the couple have been seeing each other on a regular basis for months or even longer before making a commitment to each other. In times past, the search for and obtaining the consent for marriage, was a more quiet and discreet affair conducted through an intermediary or a matchmaker. Only the immediate individuals involved—the young man, his intermediary/matchmaker and the prospective bride and her parents—were privy to the fact that negotiations for marriage were on hand. Once agreements for the marriage were made, a small party was held to celebrate and officially announce the betrothal. The engagement celebration was usually held on a Saturday evening at the home of the bride and was as small or as large an affair as the couple desired it to be. The betrothal was considered to be a very serious event, synonymous with being married.

A very ancient tradition, one that took place before rings became popular, called for the blessing of joined hands over a loaf of bread. This symbolic rite was called *zrękowiny*, the "hand binding" ceremony, and was common among both the rich and the poor. In this tradition, the acting master of ceremonies, usually a trusted friend, uncle, or someone who was involved in helping to make the match, would ask the couple to join their hands together over a loaf of bread placed on a table. The table was covered with the best white tablecloth in the house. Their hands were then bound together with an embroidered towel made specially for the occasion. If a special cloth had not been embroidered, their hands were bound together with the finest linen cloth the home had to offer. This ceremony had a very symbolic meaning, indicating the willingness of both parties to be married and share their lives and duties. With the couple's hands clasped together, the master of ceremonies would make a small speech:

Master of ceremonies: "Two hands joined together over a loaf of bread—that is the most beautiful sign of togetherness and the happy joining of two people traveling the same road. Two hands joined together until death do them part."

If this ceremony seems a bit unusual or final, it must be remembered that at one time, the engagement ceremony was just as binding as any official marriage ceremony. The special cloth was saved in the dowry chest throughout the couple's lifetime.

In later years the engagement was an equally serious affair, except that joining hands over bread gradually disappeared as an engagement custom. A gathering of family and friends from both sides was still the norm, but the newly engaged woman now received a ring. On a table covered with a tablecloth, there was a crucifix, a small bowl with holy water, a sprinkler and the engagement ring. In the upper echelons of society in the seventeenth century, a signet ring with the family crest, which served as both her engagement and wedding ring, was given to the prospective bride at the time of the engagement.

Once everyone had arrived, the couple and guests gathered around the table. The man who was instrumental in their meeting or even the man who will act as best man to the groom is essentially the master of ceremonies. He asks them two very important questions before the witnesses:

Best Man: " Are you here of your own free will?" (The couple answers in the affirmative).

Best Man: " Have you come here with the consent of the family?"

If the answer was again in the affirmative, he blessed the engagement ring by sprinkling it with the holy water and saying "In the name of the Father, the Son and the Holy Ghost." The groom then took the ring and placed it on the finger of his bride-to-be.

From the most ancient of times, it has been the norm to seal the engagement with the presentation of a gift, deemed valuable by both parties, from the young man to the prospective bride. It could have been a fine horse, a bolt of cloth, or a pelt of fur. The young woman's acceptance of the gift was also a symbol of her agreement to unite in marriage.

The nobility wooed their brides-to-be with precious gifts of spices, jewels and other costly household goods. In 1814, it was customary among fashionable society for a man to present his fiancée with a pair of gloves. In the small villages of Śląsk, the tradition was for the young man to give his intended bride a prayer book bound in dark leather, which she carried to the altar on her wedding day. The middle merchant class presented horses, gowns, garments, as well as jewels, at the time of engagement. Very traditional among all classes of the Polish population were gifts of fabric and new shoes. The bride-to-be sometimes reciprocated by presenting her fiancé with a beautifully embroidered handkerchief or wedding shirt.

Engagement Rings and Wedding Rings

We have come to associate engagements with the young woman receiving a ring. However, when we consider the antiquity of the custom of men and women going through a prescribed set of rituals to be united as one, engagement rings are a relatively new invention. In older days, most agreements to be married were verbal ones, sealed with the transfer of goods or money and witnessed by others.

For many, many centuries, both in Poland and throughout most of Europe, engagements were as binding as the marriage ceremony itself. In fact, if a woman had engaged herself to a man who was then killed before the marriage vows took place, she was considered a widow and not a single woman. By the same token, there was little difference between an engagement ring and a wedding ring for many centuries. On agreeing to marry, the woman received a ring and it was the only one she received. Then, in 12 A.D., Pope Innocent II declared that weddings must take place in churches and that a waiting period must be observed between engagement and marriage. This led to the custom of a separate wedding ring.

As a symbol of engagement, the diamond has endured over the centuries. It has been the most popular stone for engagement rings and was reputedly first worn in medieval Italy. The fashion for diamonds as an engagement ring was observed even in Poland. The engagement ring of Queen Bona Sforza, the Italian princess who married the Polish King Zygmunt 1 (1467-1548), was a large diamond. Unable to find a suitably large diamond in his coffers, Zygmunt bid his minions to travel to Vienna and Italy to find the ring that he felt would appeal to his intended. It was subsequently bought in Vienna. The ring was set in a gold band and carried a Latin inscription on the inside: BENEDICAT TE DEUS ET CRESCERE FACIAT IN GENTEM MAGNUM(May God bless you and make you grow into a great nation). Over the centuries, however, Polish women have received engagement rings that consisted of a variety of precious and semi-precious stones.

Polish craftsmen were working precious metals and stones into objects of unparalleled beauty in the city of Cracow from the time of the Middle Ages. Goldsmiths and jewelers settling in Cracow, from Germany, Italy, Holland and Hungary, fashioned exquisite rings, bracelets, earrings, gold chains, brooches and clasps. Diamonds, pearls, sapphires, rubies, emeralds, garnets, amethysts, as well as almadines, turquoise, coral, carnelians, jasper, and gold were imported in substantial amounts to make whatever jewelry a woman might desire. Some stones were associated with certain beliefs and extraordinary powers. For instance, it was believed that amethysts protected the wearer against drunkenness. Chrysolite chased away nightmares. Pearls helped to relieve melancholy, while garnets gave joy to the heart and topaz soothed anger.

When Józef Chełmonski, one of Poland's most famous nineteenth century painters, married Maria Szymanowska in 1878, the engagement ring was a sapphire surrounded by diamonds. Another famous Pole, Jarosław Dąbrowski, during his military marriage to his sweetheart, gave her a garnet marquise.

Wedding rings came into fashion very slowly and even then mostly among the wealthy, where another ring of silver or gold was not beyond their means. This was an influence brought to Poland from the west. We know, for instance, that when Marie-Casimir d'Arquien married Jan Zamoyski in 1665, she received a wedding ring.

Katarzyna Jagiellon, daughter of King Zygmunt I and Bona Sforza, married John II Vasa, Duke of Finland and King of Sweden in 1562. When his enemies threatened her and asked her to make a choice between leaving her husband or suffering dungeons and death with him, Katarzyna removed her wedding ring and showed the Latin words inscribed inside: NEMO NISI MORS i.e, only death will part us. The year of their marriage was also inscribed.

"Hand in Hand" wedding ring, c. 1700.

A pair of clasped hands is one of the oldest symbols of plighted troth. A particular set of wedding rings dating from the Renaissance period in Poland was termed the "hand in hand" setting. As a wedding ring it shows up in the last will and testament of many Polish individuals in the seventeenth century. This was a beautifully crafted gold engagement and wedding ring which, when fitted together on the finger revealed two hands clasped together as a symbol of the marriage union. The inscription inside read SI DEUS PRONOBIS QUIS CONTRA NOS (If God for us, who against us). This ring later became a single ring with a wide band, with the two hands clasped together on the surface, and was crafted either in silver or in gold. By the eighteenth century, wedding rings became more and more common. Other rings were inscribed with: *Serce moje i twoje, Połlcz Boże oboje*(My heart and yours, join together, Lord). Sometimes the inscription was as simple as the names or initials of the couple along with the date and year of the wedding.

The finger upon which the wedding ring is placed is full of symbolism. In the sixth century, St. Isidore of Sevile taught that the groom gave his bride a ring as a sign of mutual love, and placed it on fourth finger of the left hand (the thumb being the first) because of the belief that a vein in that finger led directly to the heart. This idea stemmed from even more ancient times when Egyptian anatomists recorded the belief that a certain delicate nerve passed from the fourth finger to the heart. This belief spread with Christianity to almost every civilized country. However, during the fifteenth century, in certain ecclesiastical regions in Europe, the wedding ring was placed upon the fourth finger of the bride's right hand. According to historians, the custom of wearing the ring on the left hand changed to wearing it on the right hand during the time of the Reformation. The tradition of wearing one's wedding ring on the fourth finger of the right hand continued in many countries of Eastern Europe and the Mediterranean. Like the Greeks, Russians and Ukranians, the majority of couples married in Poland wore their wedding rings on the fourth finger of the right hand.

Another major change in wedding ring customs has to do with the placing of the ring on the finger during the ceremony. It is customary during marriage ceremonies today for the wedding ring to be placed directly upon the fourth finger of the left hand. Up until the time of the sixteenth century, the ring was moved from finger to finger while slowly invoking the Trinity. At the words "In the name of the Father" the ring was placed on the top of the thumb. On saying "In the name of the Son" the groom moved the ring to the top of the forefinger, then to the top of the middle finger on saying "and of the Holy Ghost." Finally the ring was slipped on the fourth finger and left in place on the closing word "Amen." This is such a lovely action that it seems unbelievable that the tradition has been lost.

Young couples today are looking for a more unique and personal statement when it comes to choosing engagement and wedding rings. Besides those already mentioned, there are two very beautiful and unique choices for settings for engagement and wedding rings that have centuries-old traditions in Poland: amber and coral.

Coral is a stone that occurs only in warm seas such as the Mediterranean, Malaysian and Japanese waters. Some of the finest stones are dredged off the coast of Algiers and Tunisia. Despite its name, coral ranges from snow white to red to black. There are numerous shades in between including salmon, pale pink, bright rose and ox-blood red. Being firm, yet soft, coral is a stone that can easily be tooled into various shapes for rings, cameos and beads. Coral is a very appropriate choice for wedding rings, necklaces and earrings because of the ancient belief that the red color of coral protected the bride against the evil eye.

Amber is another very popular and traditional stone in Poland. Found along the southern coast of the Baltic sea, amber comes from the resin of amber pine (*Pinus succinifera*) that grew in forests over fifty million years ago. It can also be found in the countries along the Baltic Sea such as Estonia, Latvia and Lithuania. Over time the trees became buried, and because of heat and pressure, the resin they exuded became solidified as amber. Insects that existed in the climate and often sat on trees or bark fissures, were frequently imprisoned in the gluey resin and can be seen trapped within the solid amber. In the Baltic region, amber is commonly thrown back by the sea on sandy shores after rough weather, or mined along the shoreline. Inland it occurs in regions containing bluish clay and alluvial soils with beds of lignite. Pieces containing insects such as ants, bees, beetles, flies, etc. are highly valued. This lustrous fossil ranges in colors from transparent golden to yellow brown, to orange and red brown. Amber is soft enough to be cut and carved into various shapes for settings of rings, beads for necklaces, as well as other jewelry. It is now mined in Poland in areas where amber pine trees are known to have existed, such as the Kurpie region which at one time consisted of vast tracts of forests. It is also collected from the beds of small streams and from sea cliffs. Beads, pendants, rings and figurines have been carved from amber for thousands of years. The ancient trades routes of Europe carried large amounts of this unusual fossil that resembles a gem. At one time, amber was considered as precious as gold and bartered for other goods such as copper, iron and bronze. It was also thought to have magic and healing properties against arthritis and rheumatism.

Any reputable jeweler who sells gems and settings will create a setting for you. Remember that in the past, all precious and semiprecious stones were regarded as appropriate for wedding rings. It is only recently that diamonds have gained prominence. Even queens have chosen to be married with a plain hoop of gold. Designs include a variety of motifs.

At left, *ring designs from the eleventh to thirteenth centuries found in Gdansk.* At right, *designs popular in Poland during the Renaissance.*

Ideas to Borrow from the Past:

- Look for a jeweler who can fashion a wedding ring for you from the many designs in the illustrations. Think about choosing a coral or amber engagement ring.

- Wear your engagement and wedding rings on the right hand instead of left. Another approach is to wear a set of rings on the left and a band on the right.

- Traditionally, the wedding rings were ordered and paid for by the groom.

Bridal Attendants and Groomsmen

While parents were busy making the wedding preparations, the prospective couple—whether they were very rich or came from the humblest of homes—began to invite friends and family to the wedding and choose wedding clothes. It was a time for the prospective bride and groom to select or make appropriate engagement and wedding gifts for each other. This was also a time to choose bridal attendants and groomsmen.

The number of attendants varied from two to four attendants, with the larger wedding parties consisting of ten attendants. What is most traditional, however, is that all attendants, both male and female, were always single, unmarried individuals. The maid of honor and the best man were chosen carefully, for they became central figures in the wedding day activities. Sometimes it was the maid of honor who accompanied her friend to invite the people of the community to the wedding. Because most weddings were celebrated with numerous folk songs, the maid of honor took a lead role in singing songs during specific parts of the wedding. She also helped the bride make her bridal wreath and bridal clothes, and assisted her in getting dressed on the morning of her wedding day. It was also the role of the maid of honor to pin the groom's boutonniere on his lapel.

The groom took equal care in choosing his best man. His role was no less important than that of the maid of honor. It was often his role to personally visit the homes of the people the groom wished to invite to his nuptials. He made sure that everything ran smoothly, from getting the groom to the home of the bride early in the morning, until late the following morning when the reception finally concluded. In olden days this role of master or mistress of ceremonies was often performed by a special man or woman (or both). This individual decided when it was time to leave for the church and made sure everyone got into the right vehicles. It was he who decided when it was time for the unveiling (see *oczepiny*). And while everyone is expected to make toasts to the bride and groom, it was his role to lead the toasting. With the passage of time and the changes it generally brings, this role has been eliminated from Polish weddings and was given over to the best man. One of the key functions of the groomsmen was, of course, to partner the bridesmaids. It was a groomsman's role to dance with a bridesmaid, make sure she enjoyed herself throughout the day, and at its conclusion, to escort her home. The occasion called for all the gallantry and fulfillment of strict codes of conduct that existed between men and women of the earlier centuries.

Polish folk legends offer insight into the role of groomsmen on a wedding day. According to these legends, the reason a groom is surrounded by so many men on the day of his wedding has its origins in the days of bold knights and fair ladies. At one time a Polish knight was traveling to meet his bride for their wedding day. Accompanying him were his fellow knights who were to act as his groomsmen. As they neared their destination they were set upon by a small army of his enemies, which he and his knights valiantly fought and defeated. From that time on, the groom always had enough men with him to make sure nothing interfered with meeting his bride on the appointed day.

Wedding Invitations

Long ago when the world was a smaller place and people married within their own towns and villages, inviting guests to a wedding was a much simpler affair. Sometimes the bridegroom himself, or both the bride and groom, visited the individuals they wished to have attend the wedding and personally extended invitations. Another approach was to have two of the groomsmen dress up in their Sunday best, mount horses that were decorated with flowers, and call on each of the guests personally to extend invitations on behalf of the parents and the engaged couple. Around 1910, the custom of sending out invitations began among the minor gentry. Initially, they were handed out by a special person going from home to home or the next village, either on foot or horseback. By the beginning of 1918, invitations were being sent out by mail, first among the wealthy and then by all classes of people. Today, mailed wedding invitations are a necessity. They should compliment your wedding style and act as a precursor to the wedding festivities. Your wedding invitations can be as expressive of your style as the rest of your wedding.

Many individuals have researched their family's roots and have found ties with the minor and major nobility of Poland. Most families had a motto, family coat-of-arms, or a crest that was handed down through the generations or was developed as families made alliances under very unusual circumstances. Take, for instance, the romantic story of the Ogończyk family.

According to legend, the year is 1252, when knights were bold and brave and rescued damsels in distress. A town in Poland was under attack by a horde of pagan heathens, who were pillaging and plundering the town of its wealth and killing its citizens. As Polish knights engaged the enemy in combat, the air was filled with the sound of swords clashing and men screaming and fighting. Amidst the dust and confusion of the battle, a knight, by the name of Peter, spied a beautiful young maiden being carried off on horseback by one of the heathens. The young maiden had her arms outstretched in his direction in silent supplication for him to save her. The young knight spurred his horse into action, caught and slayed the enemy and safely carried the young maiden to a spot away from the fighting. The maiden, the daughter of the wealthy Odrowlż family, immediately fell in love with her rescuer and offered herself to him. As a symbol of her sincerity, she took off one of her rings, broke it in half and gave it to him, saying that she would wait for him to come and claim her and make her his wife. The knight, somewhat taken aback by this declaration from a

31

Crest of the Ogończyk family: a white half ring and an arrow on a red field beneath a crown with two hands raised in supplication.

comely maiden in the midst of a heated battle, tucked the ring away and returned to the scene of fighting.

The maiden, the daughter of a wealthy nobleman, was returned to the safety of the castle. She said nothing of her rescue to her family. As was the manner of the times, the family eventually began making plans for her marriage. Arrangements were made for suitors to be brought to the castle for the family's perusal as a suitable husband for their daughter. The maiden, carefully nurturing her secret love, kept putting them off and continuously looked out the castle windows for her rescuer to appear. After months of waiting, the maiden began to despair and could no longer put her parents off. She agreed to a marriage. On her wedding day, just as she was to approach the altar, her secret knight arrived. Peter brought forth the half ring that his betrothed had given him and claimed her for his own. The maiden begged her family to allow her to keep her promise. After hearing the entire story, the family agreed to the marriage. On the day of their wedding, Peter Ogończyk and his young bride developed a new family coat-of-arms. It consisted of a white half ring and an arrow on a red shield. Their personal crest, on top of a knight's helmet, was two hands raised up in supplication in memory of the maiden begging to be rescued.

If you have a family crest or coat-of-arms, or you want to adopt one, this is a good time to do so. You may want to use a crest in some way as part of your invitations. If you do not have a family crest, motto or coat of arms, you can use the crest of Polish kings—a crowned white eagle on a red field—as the background for your invitation. A combination of an American flag with a Polish flag could also be used.

Cracow: blue field, red facade, raised portcullis reveals white eagle with gold crown and talons.

Warsaw:mermaid on red field holds gold sword and yellow shield, topped by yellow crown.

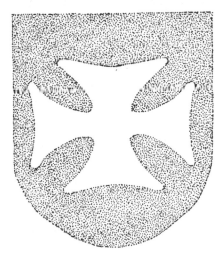

Zakopane: blue field cut by white triangle with green tree stump; backed by dredge once used to pull out stumps.

Rzeszów: silver maltese cross on blue field; in ancient times field was red.

National emblem of Poland: crowned white eagle on red field.

Gdańsk: red field with two maltese crosses topped by gold crown.

Crests of the different regions of Poland.

Many Polish cities also have their own crest. For example, Warsaw has the Water Maiden or Siren. Cracow, the original capital of Poland, has a castle with the crowned Polish eagle at its gates. If you know from which city or region in Poland your family originates, you might want to use one of the illustrations of crests located in this book. Most printers will be happy to work with you. Remember that the national colors of the Polish flag are red and white. The colors are often used on stationary and as the color theme for dinners and special occasions.

Another very beautiful approach to invitations may be to have them printed in both Polish and English, with the information written in English on one side and in Polish on the other.

Using a Polish love poem or a quote from a Polish love poem on your invitations would also be a unique approach. Choose any of the quotes used throughout this book or find others that you would prefer.

Polish-American wedding invitation, 1914.

Chapter II

Bridal Flowers

"For whom have I, with tender care,
Prepared this wreath of blossoms fair?
For thee, my love, whom I adore
As ne'er I loved a lad before."

"Song of the Fourth Maiden"
Jan Kochanowski (1530-1584)

*F*lowers and herbs have been an important part of wedding celebrations for centuries, and Poland has its own very rich and ancient herb and flower traditions.

One of Poland's oldest chroniclers, a man by the name of Kosmus, lived and wrote during the time of Poland's first king, Mieszko I (960 A.D.). When the king married a princess by the name of Dobrawa, he documented that "she placed upon her head the wreath of a girl." Wearing a wreath on one's wedding day is a Polish tradition that was continued for over a thousand years. In days of old, it was customary for young, unmarried girls to wear wreaths in their hair for almost all special occasions—going to church on Sunday and attending local dances and church fairs. The wreath was a symbol of the unmarried, virginal state. Just as clothes could identify a person's occupation and wealth, a wreath worn by a girl identified her as someone who was single and available for marriage. This was common practice among both the privileged nobility and common folk.

The importance of the wreath is evident throughout the life of the young girl. It continues through courtship and culminates with the last moments of her wedding day. It is reflected in numerous songs that are sung to and about young women as they reach marriageable age. By far the most important wreath a Polish girl would wear would be her wedding wreath, composed of specific flowers, herbs and ribbons. The wreath is central to specific rites such as the maiden evening where the young bride weaves a wreath for her wedding day in the company of her attendants. It is also the central focus of a song sung during the blessing of the bride by her parents:

"Błogosławcie jajcowie
Ostatni wianek na głowie
Błogosławcie ją sąsiedzi
Dopóki tutaj siedzi
Błogosławcie ją drużbowie i druchneczki
Ostani wianek na głowie.

Bestow your blessings, father
The last wreath on her head
Bestow your blessings, neighbors
while she still sits here.
Bestow your blessings, groomsmen and bridesmaids
The last wreath on her head.

The Maiden Evening

The gathering of women to celebrate, adorn and advise a bride before her wedding is as ancient a custom as marriage itself. In Poland, a special event, called the maiden evening, was set aside for just this purpose. It took place the evening before the wedding. The bride-to-be met with her bridesmaids to decorate the house for the next day's festivites, make boutonnieres for the groom and groomsmen, and help with the cooking if need be. But the most important reason for getting together was for the single girls to officially say goodbye to their friend as a single woman and to help her make the bridal wreath to wear on her wedding day.

The evening began by covering the table with a white tablecloth. The prospective bride brought herbs and flowers from her garden to weave her wreath. From the most ancient of times, young Polish women of all economic classes tended flower gardens where they grew their favorite flowers. Hollyhocks, asters, nasturtium, pansies, larkspur, violets, lilies, lovage, mint, rue, myrtle, rosemary, lavender, and roses were all lovingly tended in preparation for their own marriage or those of their friends. The bride herself or the maid of honor fastened the herbs and flowers around a circular base made from a tender branch or a metal ring.

There were five herbs that played the most significant roles in the bridal hair wreaths of Polish brides. These were rue, rosemary, lavender, myrtle, and periwinkle. Of these, rue (*Ruta graveolens*) was by far the most favored and preferred herb in wedding customs. It was considered the herb of unmarried girls. To see rue growing in a garden was to know that some young woman was preparing for her wedding day. Rue figured significantly in all aspects of marriage, such as fortunetelling and marriage predictions, courtship rituals and engagements. In medieval times, a young woman gave a suitor a wreath of rue as a way of confirming a marriage agreement. There was also a time when, instead of rings, wreaths of rue were exchanged by a young couple at a wedding ceremony. Rue was also used to decorate the wedding cake, the hats of the groomsmen and even the whip for the horses that pulled the carriage carrying the bride to church on her wedding day. As a talisman for young, unmarried girls, rue had no equal, to the point where, should a young girl die unmarried, a wreath of rue was added to her coffin.

Rosemary (*Rosmarinus officinalis*), with its spicy fragrance and soft blue flowers, is another plant that played an important part in Polish weddings. From time immemorial, rosemary has been known as the plant of fidelity, and was linked with weddings and bridal wreaths. In one of his epic poems, Polish poet, Juliusz Słowacki, has Aldona say to Dowmunt, "I'm going to be married. I will don a wreath on my forehead...some wild roses and much rosemary; may they foretell my happiness." In 1692, Stanisław Wierzbowski, who left a detailed account of his marriage, stated that on the eve of his marriage he sent his beloved a rosemary plant as a symbol of his eternal and unfailing love. Hundreds of Polish folk songs also testify to its importance on this particular day.

"When you win my love
You will have my hand
And a garland of rosemary
From my garden fair.

I shall offer it
To you my dear love
I shall place it on the altar
At the wedding mass."
—Polish folk song

Rosemary was especially popular as part of the wedding flower tradition in the Poznań region of Poland. The bride, as well as the bridesmaids, wore wreaths of rosemary on their heads. During the engagement period, the young man wore a branch of rosemary tied with a green ribbon in his cap. This was prepared for him by his fiancée. Over time, the rosemary was tied with a white ribbon and pinned to the lapel instead of the cap.

Long ago, during a Poznań wedding, the priest placed small wreaths of rosemary on the heads of the couple as a symbol of their fidelity to each other instead of wedding rings.

Lavender (*Lavandula officinalis*) was a favorite for bridal wreaths in the regions associated with Great Poland. It, too, is encountered in poetry and folk songs throughout the centuries.

"Wianku mój, wianku
Wianku lawendowy
Musis ustępować czepuskowki z głowy."

My wreath, my wreath
My lavender wreath
You must be replaced by a cap.

Another song claims:
Mój wianku lewandowy
Zdejmuję cię z mojej głowy.

My lavender wreath
I'm removing from my head.

Lavender was widely grown in gardens and enjoyed tremendous popularity, not only as a plant used in bridal customs, but also as a strewing herb and an herb to place in chests and coffers between sheets and special occasion clothes.

If a girl knew she was going to be married during the winter months, she took special care to have periwinkle (*Vinca minor*) in her garden. Periwinkle is a trailing groundcover which remains green during the winter months. She protected the plants against freezing during these cold months by lightly covering it with straw.

A plant that became prominent in Polish wedding traditions during the period between the two world wars was myrtle(*Myrtus communis*). In Polish, the plant is called *mirt*. This myrtle was a shrubby plant grown indoors on windowsills as a potted plant, and tended very carefully by single girls of marriageable age. It was used exclusively or in conjunction with rue and rosemary for the bridal wreath. A careful study of old photographs, such as one of a Polish-American couple from Niagara Falls, New York, shows brides with sprigs of myrtle on the hemline of their wedding dresses and/or along the edges of their veils. Myrtle was also used to decorate the wedding cake and the hats of the groomsmen. The groom's boutonniere, as well as those of the groomsmen, were made from myrtle and tied with a white ribbon. This practice was especially common

Bridal photo of Aniela Wieczorek and Józef Dera on May 12, 1913, at Niagara Falls, New York. Bridal veil is decorated with myrtle (Myrtus communis). **Photo courtesy of Brian Stanish and Mrs Emily Stanish.**

41

Bridal photo of Sharon Leonard Kiefer, 1991. Wreath of myrtle, rosemary and roses is worn over the veil.

in the southern mountain regions of Poland.

In very old Polish weddings, the above mentioned herbs were fashioned into simple green wreaths without other adornment. With the passage of time, however, the wreath began to change. Flowers were added to the simple greenery. Real flowers, especially in the dead of winter, could only be had by the very rich who owned hothouses.

Orange blossoms have also played a role in old Polish wedding traditions. Orange blossoms, a traditional wedding flower that was used in England, became fashionable among the wreaths of wealthy brides. The orange blossom is said to symbolize virginity and the promise of fecundity. The white blossoms are a symbol of innocence and purity while the orange tree has a reputation of bearing abundant fruit, and it is hoped that the bride who wears it will have similar fruitfulness.

It is believed that the Moors first introduced the orange tree into Spain, where it was much prized and considered a rarity. According to legend the orange tree belonging to the King of Spain was coveted by the French ambassador. He knew that the gardener's daughter longed to marry, but couldn't because of lack of a dowry. The ambassador approached her and offered her a generous dowry in return for a cutting from the prized orange tree. She agreed to the plan and obtained a cutting without being detected. On her wedding day, wishing to honor the tree that had brought her happiness, she wove a circlet of orange blossoms and wore it in her raven hair. The custom passed from Spain to France, from France to England and eventually reached Poland.

For a more simple country wedding, whatever sweet smelling flowers were blooming in the garden and countryside were appropriate for incorporating into the wreaths and bridal bouquets. Roses, especially white ones, were very popular among the rich and poor alike. Lilies were also a perennial favorite. Roses were most popular in the Mazowse region among a group of people who called themselves Kurpie. In Poland, as elsewhere, roses symbolize love, and lilies innocence and faithfulness.

If real flowers were unavailable, crepe paper flowers were cleverly fashioned into morning glories and lily-of-the-valley. In the Kaszuby region in northern Poland, a wreath of bilberry (whortelberry, huckleberry) with yellow paper roses was very popular. When artificial silk flowers became available, they, too, were used in making the bridal wreath, especially if the wedding was a winter one and fresh flowers were hard to come by. Following the addition of flowers, either real or artificial, were strings of pearls, or gold and silver braiding that was entwined around the wreath. Also very popular was the addition of long cascades of ribbons that were attached to the back of the wreath, and flowed down to the small of the back, sometimes reaching all the way to the floor.

When veils began to become popular as a part of wedding attire, they, too, were incorporated in Polish wedding traditions. The bride wore a veil according to the new "look" but in keeping with age old traditions, wore a wreath of herbs and flowers on top.

Central Poland had another unique custom regarding the wreath. Two wreaths of rue were woven for the bride. One was worn on her head on her wedding day and the other was used for carrying the wedding rings.

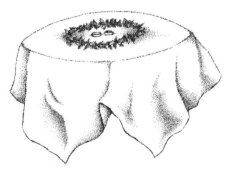

Rings were carried to the altar inside a wreath of rue on a plate covered with an embroidered cloth.

In this custom, a specially embroidered cloth was placed on an appropriately sized plate. The wreath was placed on the cloth with the two wedding rings inside the wreath. Wouldn't this be a lovely, traditional custom to revive instead of bringing the rings to the altar on a pillow?

The wedding wreath was considered very important, and after the wedding it was saved in the dowry chest and crumbled into the first bath of a new baby. The herbs were believed to have special magical powers and be helpful in treating a variety of illnesses.

The Wedding Bouquet

In very old Polish traditions, the bride did not carry flowers on her wedding day. She held a beautifully bound prayer book given to her as a gift from the groom, or perhaps a rosary. However, wedding bouquets were already fairly common in Poland at the beginning of the 1830s. A historian documenting a Polish wedding in 1830 wrote "the bride enters the carriage, holding a bouquet in her hand."

Like today, bouquets were bought from a florist or made at home from real or artificial flowers in white, cream or rose colors. These were accented with knotted ribbons that sometimes reached as far as the hem of the bride's dress. Flowers popular in the past were white—roses, carnations, lilies and the calla lily. Because many couples married in the early fall, it was also common to see spikes of grain such as wheat, oats and rye and colorful berries added to a bouquet.

Church Flowers

If you are trying to decide on a color scheme for flowers in a church, try to keep in mind that red and white are the colors of the flag of Poland. The red and white color combination is used for many official Polish functions where flowers are needed—the flowers are usually red and white carnations. In country villages, friends and family raided their gardens and the countryside to fill the church with flowers, the leaves of fruit trees, evergreens and large bunches of grain on their stalks, such as oats, wheat and rye. Your choice of flowers will be decided by your overall approach—whether it is formal, semiformal or casual. Each approach is the correct one, if that is your particular wish.

Ideas to borrow from the past

- The wonderful thing about all the traditional herbs used in Polish weddings is that they are available for purchase as plants and can be grown in one's own garden. If you have a florist who is willing to work with you, you can save costs by growing some of your own plants and delivering them to the florist to incorporate into your floral arrangements, be it a hair wreath, bouquet or boutonniere.

- Exchanging wreaths of rue, as well as rings, would give your wedding an ancient tone that would be truly unforgettable.

- A beautifully made wreath, whether from real herbs and flowers, or from artificial ones, can continue to be a joy long past the wedding day. It can be hung near your wedding portrait or somewhere in your bedroom.

- An autumn wedding can successfully incorporate grains and berries of almost any kind in headdress, bouquets and church decorations.

- According to Polish custom, the wedding flowers were paid for by the groom.

Chapter III

Wedding Clothes

I fell in love with you when you were barefoot,
wearing a crown, in the dawn, in the night.
> "I Fell in Love With You"
> Konstanty Ildefeons Gałczyński (1905-1953)

When it comes to bridal clothes, the entire fashion world is at your command. There is no end to the number of bridal salons available to select the dress that fits your notion of what you want to look like on your wedding day. You can re-create a fairy tale fantasy by wearing the grandest of ball-gown styles, with long trains and fitted bodices. You can go semiformal with a shorter hemline, train and veil. You can wear the traditional white in an unlimited number of styles and lengths. Or, you can pick a color for your wedding dress.

For the past one hundred fifty years, a young, virginal bride, dressed in white has been the predominant choice, but you need not stay within that limitation. If you have concerns about departing from the traditional white dress for your wedding, you may find encouragement in knowing that bridal dresses were not always white in the past, nor were they worn only once. That, too, is a relatively new invention. Many women used their wedding dress as their best dress for all special occasions for as long as possible. This was true in many parts of Europe including England, France and Poland.

In 1475, a Polish princess marrying a Bavarian king wore a crimson dress, completely embroidered with pearls in a flower motif. Her hair was braided with pearls, and on her head she wore a costly crown over a transparent veil.

When Austrian princess Anna Habsburg married Polish King Zygmunt II in May of 1592, she wore a dress of silver brocade. She wore her hair loose with a small green wreath on her head.

The French princess, Marie Louise de Gonzaga, second wife of King Władysław IV (1646), wore a blue dress embroidered with silver threads and silver buttons.

In the first half of the eighteenth century, Polish women of the nobility and well-to-do class, married in what was then called sack (sacque) dresses. This garment was an unbelted gown, loose from the shoulder to the floor. A fullness at the back was created by gathering the fabric at the neck band, which added to the looseness of the gown. In front, beneath a low neckline that was oval or square in shape, was a V-shaped panel of fabric (called a stomacher) that converged to a point low on the waistline. This region was highly embroidered. The necklines on sacks were usually low and oval, or square in shape to better display one's bosom and jewelry. The sleeves were tightly fitted to the elbow and had from one to three linen or lace ruffles that extended from the elbow halfway to the wrist. The lower half of the dress did not open at the front. It was simply worn over hoops and derived its elegance from the material. It was made of silver lamé, painted or printed silk and the richest brocades.

The sack dress required many yards of fabric and was sewn from the most expensive brocades. The Polish version was made of brocades in pale colors. In those days one loose sack dress required 30 to 32 yards of brocade, approximately 21 inches wide. For her wedding sack, Zofii Wodzicki of the fabulously wealthy Kasiński family, used a great many silver ribbons on white brocade for the V-shaped panel of the wedding dress.

Over time the sack dress was transformed into a pleated gown known as *á la francaise.* This was also a very loose gown, but had two layers of pleats at the back of the neckline that hung loosely all the way to the floor. In the front, too, it had a V-shaped panel of fabric but was decorated with a ladder of bows that decreased in size towards the waist. The lower half of the gown was open to reveal a petticoat. The petticoats were usually made from the same fabric as the rest of the gowns, usually giving them the appearance of being a single garment.

To have her portrait painted, Princess Izabella Czartoryski dressed herself in a magnificent sack gown with a low neckline. At her neck, instead of costly jewelry, she wore a simple bow made from the same fabric as her gown. Hairstyles to complete such an ensemble included combing the hair back from the face and arranging it in a bun at the back of the head, a chignon at the base of the neck, or a single braid.

In the nineteenth century, popular fashion magazines appeared in Poland and brought the latest fashions from France and England, which were readily adopted and copied by fashionable ladies. Among the first of such journals was *Motyl*, started in the 1820s in Warsaw. There also appeared *Dziennik Mód Paryskich*, which illustrated the latest in men's and women's fashions. It was followed by *Bluszcz*, also coming out of Warsaw. All of these journals printed color lithographs of the latest Parisian styles, including gowns from Worth. Almost everything a fashionable lady needed was imported from either the East or West. Beautiful and costly materials such as silk, brocades, damasks, satins and velvet were being imported from Turkey, Greece, and China. Beautiful cashmere shawls were brought from India via England; eventually these began to be imitated successfully and made in Poland. From the West, especially France, Holland and England, came muslins, tulles, taffetas, batistes, and patterned silks. The finest of laces were being imported from France, Belgium and Saxony.

The French Empire fashions reached Poland almost as soon as they appeared in Paris. As part of this fashion trend, Greek, Roman, Etruscan and Egyptian art was imitated in jewelry. The women wore diadems, tiaras, necklaces, earrings, brooches, rings, clasps and ornate little gold watches, adorned in motifs of leaves and flowers, hung on gold chains. Diamonds, emeralds, rubies, sapphires, garnets, turquioses and tourmalines, enamel and niello ornaments, were applied to every imaginable type of jewelry piece. Embroidery was mostly done by local seamstresses. Collars, cuffs and handkerchiefs were minutely stitched with designs of white on white or colored threads.

Wedding dress styles followed the trends coming out of Paris and London. There was much enthusiasm for all things English and anglomania found full expression in Polish dress. Over time women's dress became less extravagant. Crinolines, bustles and corsets were abandoned, as were the rich materials of which dresses had formerly been made. Instead women wore white, high waisted muslin, cambric or calico garments, with short puffy sleeves. This fashion extended to wedding garments also. The illustration depicts a Polish wedding dress from 1805. It is made of white batiste with white embroidery along the hemline.

The white wedding dress as we know it today was basically a Victorian development. In 1840, Queen Victoria of England married for love in an all-white gown with a Honiton lace veil, and changed bridal fashions forever. Traditionally, queens wore rich brocades and robes of velvet and ermine, but Queen Victoria thought white would be better. The fashion of wedding white remained popular throughout her lifetime which came to be called the Victorian period. The exciting news of the wedding and the special white bridal gown spread to America. White did not become the universal bridal color until the 1900s. Poland held on to its traditions until 1910, when white wedding dresses were seen fairly frequently. A close inspection of wedding photographs from the turn of the century, however, reveals Polish brides dressed in white gowns but still following some elements of traditional Polish dress. Their dresses and veils were covered with sprigs of myrtle, all over the veil, along the hemline and down the train of the dress.

Jewelry and Accessories

In the seventeenth century, ornaments on the wedding dresses of Polish ladies consisted of braiding, ribbons and lace trimmings. Later came the fashion for bobbin-lace and needlework lace, both imported and locally made. All accessories of ladies' dress were modeled on Western European fashions: embroidered slippers and gloves, garters with jeweled clasps, embroidered vanity-bags, colorful parasols and fans. The fans were often magnificent works of art. They were imported from abroad and made of lace, mother-of-pearl, tortoise shell, ivory or feathers from unusual birds such as peacock and ostrich. Other fans were made of splints of wood, gilded or painted, and covered with the finest parchment, silk or paper. The women also treated themselves to little gold watches imported from Paris or Vienna. They were often set with small diamonds or other stones and, as a rule, were worn on a gold chain around the neck.

Writing about women's jewelry during the reign of Polish King August III (1733-1763), a chronicler records: "The neck was decorated with coral, then coral entwined with pearls, then pearls only, then gold chains and at the last a thin black velvet ribbon to which was attached a diamond cross or a miniature portrait surrounded by costly stones. On their ears they hung small pearl or ruby earrings worked in gold and then later larger earrings in the shape of roses from either diamonds or their imitations. Later they became even larger wearing large dangling earrings made from pearls or diamonds."

On their feet, the women wore slippers made of white silk or satin covered with embroidery. They were tied to the leg with white silk or satin ribbons that crisscrossed and reached above the ankles. They were worn

Wedding dress made of batiste with detail of embroidery along the hemline, c. 1805

Parisian wedding fashions were copied in Poland. **Dziennik Mód Paryskich, 1840.**

Note ringlets at side of face and coiled braid at the back. **Dziennik Mód Paryskich, 1848.**

***Empire look in 1913. Part of an advertisement for Herseg Fashions in
Warsaw. Tygodnik Ilustrowany, 1913***

Hair and straw hat with cherries. **Bluszcz, 1882.**

Hair and hat, backview. **Bluszcz, 1875.**

Hair and hat, front view. **Bluszcz, 1875.**

Hair style with bangs. A dress made from voile. **Bluszcz, 1906.**

Hair style. **Bluszcz, 1886**

Summer hat for a young woman. **Bluszcz, 1905**

Fancy dress shoe for a woman, as advertised in Tygodnik Ilustrowany, **1894.**

over stockings of white silk or net. From Warsaw, the demand for silk and satin slippers spread all over the country, so that every female wanted a pair of silk slippers. Husbands bought them for their wives and fathers for their daughters. Single men bought them for their sweethearts, and eventually they became a required engagement present! In later years, colored satin slippers took the place of the white ones. These were without embroidery and were no longer tied to the foot with a ribbon, but with a silver clasp. This clasp was initially very small and thin, but with later trends, became so large it covered the entire front of the toes. In later years, high boots buttoned on the side became the vogue.

Garters to hold up stockings were, at first, made from ribbon. Later they were bought from a haberdasher who embroidered the ribbons with gold or silver threads. In its later evolutionary stages, the garter was held in place with a pearl clasp or buckle.

To complete ladies' ensembles were two other fashionable items: gloves and shawls. Elbow length kid gloves were *de riguer*, and often heavily embroidered with colored silk or gold threads. Fingerless mittens of lace and open work were especially popular among the gentry and country girls.

The use of white silk shawls, either square or rectangular, became very popular in the seventeenth century in Poland and continued throughout the centuries. The fashion was brought to Poland from Italy and Germany.

The shawl often had embroidered flowers, with gold thread and colored silk threads. Distinctive in the seventeenth century was a stylized carnation embroidered in the corners. This trend in silk shawls passed from the wealthy down to the middle and poorer strata of Polish society and was part of wedding dress until the nineteenth century, lasting the longest in folk costumes in the Rzeszów region. Other popular embroidery motifs on shawls were tulips, daisies, margerites and roses.

The Bridegroom and His Attendants

Men's wedding attire in Poland varied in style and ornamentation over the centuries as much as women's dress. Men essentially wore the fashionable dress of the era to match the women. Men's dress was also heavily influenced by England and France. Earlier centuries had seen evening dress complete with knee breeches and powdered hair.

Fortunately, there remain in Polish archives numerous illustrative magazines that give very accurate depictions of the fashions that were popular in Poland through the centuries. One of these illustrative magazines was *Dziennik Mód Paryskich* (Journal of Paris Fashions), which was started by a tailor by the name of Tomasz Kulczycki in 1840. It covered the latest news and information about men's and women's fashions. Most of the illustrations were colored lithographs. They were printed in one of the best printing houses of the times, and the drawings executed by a specially imported artist from Vienna by the name on Antoni Weidel.

Every issue of the magazine included men's dress and fashion. These illustrations, coupled with historical writings, leave a legacy of male fashions in Poland. In 1842, the *Journal of Paris Fashion* dictated that "the frock coat, as it is worn in the English style, is the dress of choice for ceremonial occasions." No event could be more ceremonial than a wedding and the writings of the times indicate that men took this fashion advice to heart when it came time to choose their wedding attire.

Polish costume historians have noted that frock coats were made in a wide variety of materials and colors including various shades of red, navy blue, violet and green. Waistcoats were also worn. These were short, heavily embroidered, sleeveless vests whose color harmonized with the outer coat. For special occasions, such as weddings, the waistcoats were made of silk, satin or velvet and were embroidered in gold or silver threads. Shirts were often frilled or pleated and made of muslin or batiste. The outfit was completed with a cravat or bow-tie, and even ascots were worn by some men. For instance, the description of the marriage of Helena

Men's hair and wedding attire. **Dziennik Mód Paryskich, 1840.**

Modrzejewska to Karol Chłapowski in 1868, notes that "[the groom] wore a morning coat with lapels trimmed in black velvet and had a gardenia for a boutonniere as dictated by the Paris mode." Earlier, in 1862 it was noted that "the groom wore a traditional frock coat and a shirt with an embroidered vest and for a boutonniere had a small clump of myrtle tied together with a white ribbon."

In today's terms this male attire is equivalent to the cutaway—a jacket with tails. It is usually worn with striped trousers.

The Military Man

Not to be overlooked in men's wedding attire was the military uniform. To read Polish history is to learn that there was hardly a time when the men of Poland were not called to arms to defend the nation against foreign invaders, or to lead or participate in numerous rebellions against oppressors. Many a couple had to marry quickly, without a great deal of preparation or fanfare. Such was the wedding of General Ludwik Kicki and Natalia Bisping von Gallen on a frigid January day in 1831. He was an older, seasoned military man, decorated for bravery and heroism. She was a young twenty-three year old blond, blue-eyed society miss who, according to her diary, had known and loved Ludwik all of her life. In her diary she wrote of her wedding day: "There was no time for a trousseau. I pulled a ball grown from my wardrobe. I spent the morning in church and on returning home I bustled around making arrangements for the small group that would gather for our wedding. The blessing of my grandmother gave me courage. My parents could not arrive in Warsaw on time for the wedding. I had only myself to depend on..."

Later that same day, dressed in a gown previously worn for some other societal affair, she walked down the aisle on the arm of a general who was a friend of her husband. The groom was waiting at the altar, supporting himself on two crutches.

Another documented military wedding was that of Jarosław Dąbrowski and Pelagia Pobóg-Zgliczyńska. He was one of Poland's most outstanding military leaders in the struggle for liberty against foreign domination of Poland. She was seventeen years old and as deeply patriotic as the man she chose to be her husband. They were engaged for two years, unable to marry because of his arrest for participating in revolutionary activities that promoted a free and independent Poland. During those two years, Pelagia continuously plotted and planned for his release to no avail. Finally, in a desperate attempt to free him, she appealed to the police chief to allow him to be released so that they could marry. Historians wrote: "On April 5, 1864, in a room generally used for court martials, Jarosław Dąbrowski stood before a chaplain in his captain's uniform with his saber at his side and said his vows to his bride. There were only twenty people to witness the event, the majority of whom were fellow officers who came from all parts of the city when they heard of the event. At the conclusion of the wedding, the officers gave them a military salute. There was a small reception and the leftover food of wine and cake was sent to the jailers. You could hear their toasts and singing late into the night."

The next day Pelagia herself was arrested and jailed. Incriminating evidence had been found in their home. The story, however, ends well. Pelagia is released. While being transported to Siberia to serve time for his supposed criminal activities, her husband manages to escape. With the help of false passports, they make their way to Scandinavia and later to Paris, where they raise three sons.

Rich with ritual and dignity, the elegance of a military wedding leaves a lasting impression. A military wedding ceremony procedure does not actually exist. The ceremony is performed by a clergy member of your choice in the chapel on base. The chaplain can be dressed in religious attire or in uniform. A groom in any branch of military service, whether an enlisted man or an officer, may be married in uniform. Swords and sabers, however, are carried only by officers in full dress uniform.

The highlight of the ceremony is the Arch of Swords done by the Navy and Marine Corps, or the Arch of Sabers done by the Army and Air Force branches of the military. After the ceremony, when the bride and groom are exiting the church, the ushers, who are also in full uniform complete with swords or sabers, face each other and raise their swords to form an arch that the bride and groom pass through. This is a spectacular drama, joining the full pageantry of the military with the beauty and splendor of the wedding ritual.

After a military wedding in Warsaw, many couples made a special trip to the Tomb of the Unknown Soldier or some other special military statue where they placed a wreath of flowers in memory of the fallen soldiers and heroes.

The following are excerpts of descriptions of the weddings of some of Poland's most influential and notable individuals over the past two centuries. They are prime examples of the wide range of clothes, jewelry and flowers that were part of Polish weddings.

Wedding Dress of the Rich and Famous

The marriage of Zygmunt Krasiński, ranked as one Poland's greatest poets, and Eliza Branicka on July 26, 1843:

"(she wore)...a simple wreath of myrtle, a white satin dress with inserts of rich lace...costly jewels and diamonds accented the loveliness. He wore a frock coat. They traveled by rail to his ancestral home in Opinogóra where they were greeted by the villagers who had strewn flowers on the road."

The marriage of Maria Wasiłkowska and Jarosław Konopnicki in 1862:

"The wedding dress was tightly fitted at the waist with a wide skirt fitted over a whalebone hoop with lace ruffles at the bottom. Her hair was combed high and crowned with a wreath of live myrtle and artificial orange blossoms. It fitted over a cascade of tulle that reached to the floor. The bouquets were of daisies, gardenias and carnations surrounded with lace, and had long, wide velvet ribbons streaming down beneath the bouquet."

The marriage of Helena Modrzejewska, Poland's most famous dramatic actress, to Karol Chłapowski in 1868 at the church of St. Anne in Crakow:

"The bride wore a light blue hat with a face veil and carried a bouquet of white camellias surrounded with lace."

The marriage of Józef Chełmonski, one of Poland's great nineteenth century painters, to Maria Szymanowska in 1878:

"Her dress was from Herseg's. She was dressed in white with a long train, her hair pulled away from her face in a large chignon. Józef brought her a large, round bouquet of white roses surrounded by lace. Her attendants were her sister, dressed in a light blue dress, and her cousin, in a pale pink dress. The engagement ring was a sapphire surrounded by diamonds. There was an elegant reception and at 10 P.M. the bride went home to change. The sixty wedding guests saw them off as they left for a wedding trip to Paris."

The marriage of Marii Wandy Młodnicki and Wacław Jan Wolski in 1894:

"The wedding toilet was sewn according to the dictates of the fashions of the 1890s. The bride wore a dress with a fitted bodice with white buttons and a veil with a long train trimmed with flounces that was carried by two small attendants. Her wonderful long black

"Princess" dress made from tulle, lace and lily-of-the-valley, extending over shoulders. Lily-of-the-valley adorn the hair. Bluszcz, 1875.

Ballgown made from faille. **Bluszcz, 1887.**

Woolen walking dress for honeymoon. **Bluszcz, 1882.**

Dress for young lady. **Bluszcz, 1888.**

Dress for 7- to 9-year-old girl. **Bluszcz, 1882**

hair, which could not be fitted under her wreath of orange blossoms that had arrived only that morning from Rome in a special water container, was brought forward across her bodice in two long braids. Reaching down to her knees they contrasted beautifully with her white dress. Her mother, a beautiful woman in her own right, wore a dress of ribbed silk in a pale lilac color....Seventy people sat down at the wedding reception."

Country Wedding Dress

This chapter on wedding clothes and accessories would be incomplete without discussing the wedding attire of those individuals who were not of the ruling classes and nobility. The majority of the people of Poland were individuals who lived and worked the land as local gentry and country farmers.

Marriages in the small country villages of Poland were different only in scale and expenditure. The true issues at stake in a marriage ceremony—the public recognition of the transition of men and women from a single to married state, the approval by parents of the union, the witnessing and sanctioning of the wedding by the community—were essentially the same. Like today, the bride and groom tried to have a wedding that was commensurate with their position and standing in the community. They wore their very best clothes, often making these themselves, or commissioning a brand new set of clothes from a tailor or seamstress that would last them throughout their lifetimes. It would be their best dress for all church holy days as well as the seasonal holidays for years to come.

According to ethnographers, the years 1850 to 1890, just preceding the massive immigration of Poles to America, were the years during which the popularity of Polish folk dress peaked. The clothes worn were testimony to an individual's wealth, social and marital status, and affiliation with a town or region. Soon after this period, folk dress began to be abandoned, and even the remote country villages became influenced by city dress. The biggest advocates for maintaining group identity were found among the clergy. A pastor in the Łódź region by the name of Father Aleksander Rotyński (1880-1903) would not agree to marry a young couple if they came to church without their traditional folk dress.

According to Polish ethnographers, there are an estimated fifty different regional costumes. It is impossible within the scope of this book to cover all the various regions and the many variations in folk dress. However, I offer here the most widely known and recognized Cracow costume. It is

71

now considered the national costume, and anyone, from any region of Poland, can wear it and still be appropriately and authentically dressed.

In studying the folk dress of the various regions of Poland, it becomes clear that the traditional dress of the bride consisted of four important elements: a blouse, skirt, apron and vest. For the young man about to be married, the most important items of clothing were a shirt, pants, vest, and hat or cap. There was additional clothing for inclement weather such as coats and jackets, but for the purposes of this book, the focus will be on these four most basic and important items, as well as the small accessories that completed an ensemble.

Cracow Folk Dress

The peasant costume of the Cracow region is among the most attractive and most famous of regional Polish folk dress.

The blouse worn by a young bride was white, made of homespun linen and, in later years, of cotton, and reached down to the hips. Long sleeved and loose fitting, either with or without a collar, a slit at the neck allowed the blouse to be pulled on over the head more easily and gathered at the waist. These blouses were heavily embroidered on the collar, neck, front, shoulders, and cuffs. The blouse was tucked into the skirt.

Women's Vests

The most beautiful item of dress in the women's costume was a short-waisted vest or bodice. It was sleeveless, cut low in the front in a large U shape, and was secured together in the front with hooks and eyes. The older vests were made from green, blue or black wool and later from patterned satin, damask and paisley fabrics. These earlier vests had simple adornments of two or three rows of small pearl buttons running vertically along the two front sides near the hooks and eyes. Next to them, also running vertically, were tassels from red, green or sometimes, yellow silk. These vests were gradually enriched with colored braiding along all the outer edges. In later years, the cloth of choice for making vests was velvet, in light or dark blue, green, red and black colors. At the same time, decorations on the vest became increasingly more beautiful and lavish. Both the front and back became heavily embroidered in flower motifs either with thread or mother-of-pearl buttons, bugle beads, round beads and sequins. For wedding vests, the preferred colors were black or a deep red. Black velvet was preferred to show off the splendid colors of the beadwork and embroidery. To hide the stitchery on the inner side of the

Blouse worn by country bride in Cracow region.

velvet, the vest was usually lined in some complimentary color. A black vest was also a sharp contrast to the white of the wedding skirt and blouse.

Women's Skirts

Instead of a one-piece dress, a country girl often wore a white skirt and white blouse on her wedding day. The older skirts of the Cracow region had at one time been completely white, but with the advent of machine-made fabrics, skirts began to be made in various colorful prints and calicos. With the advent of aniline dyes, flowered skirts of ankle or tea-length came in green, red, white, blue or red. The most favored skirt had a green, blue, red or white background with large vivid flowers. It had a full gathered skirt, ankle or tea-length, that tied at the waist in the back. For weddings, the older, traditional white skirt, with lace or white-on-white embroidery remained popular for a long time. Underneath the bride wore a white slip with a great deal of embroidery along the hemline.

Apron

It was rare indeed for a Cracovian maiden to appear in public without an apron. For special occasions such as a wedding, the apron was white and made of some lightweight fabric such as cotton or tulle. Large enough to cover the front and back of the skirt, it was embroidered along the hemline about twenty inches deep in white thread. The designs for the embroidery were generally developed by the young bride herself.

Accessories

In cool weather, a large shawl was thrown over the shoulders and, if need be, pulled over the head. There were two types of shawls in this region. One was called a *rańtuch*. It was rectangular in shape, approximately 23 to 24 inches wide and 80 inches long and made at home on a loom of linen or wool. Solid in color, the edges were often embroidered or embellished with lace. In later years they were also made of lightweight tulle and also embroidered by hand.

Another type of shawl was a square shawl that was folded diagonally. For cold weather, the shawl was thicker and made of wool. For summertime, shawls were of a lighterweight fabric. These shawls were rarely in a solid color but always in large flowered prints with white or green backgrounds. This style of shawl was also extremely popular in a paisley print. Many of the paisley prints were imported from Austria and Czechoslovakia. Black or red boots, sometimes laced with colored ribbon and reaching about halfway up the calf, completed the outfit.

Shoes in black or red worn by country bride.

Hair styles of the country bride.

Jewelry

While the women of rank and wealth changed their attire daily depending on what was fashionable, country girls remained faithful to tradition the longest. Strings of coral were the most sought after type of jewelry, and every young girl dreamed of wearing at least one strand of coral on her wedding day. A coral necklace was frequently passed down from mother to daughter on the day of her wedding.

The necklaces consisted of an uneven number of strands of coral—either one, three or five strands. The latter was considered a true sign of wealth. The center coral for the longest strand was often as large as a hickory nut. The necklace was tied at the back of the neck into a bow with a red ribbon that often hung all the way to the waist. The rich wore real coral and those who couldn't afford it wore imitation strands.

Hair

Most young girls in Poland kept their hair long and braided into two long plaits. In the older days, a young bride wore her hair in braids hanging down her back, with numerous ribbons woven into the braids. On her head she wore a wreath made of rue, carnations, tulips and gillyflowers, that rested on her forehead. If it was wintertime, the bride and her bridesmaids made artificial flowers to imitate real flowers and added sequins and silver threads to make the wreath sparkle. At the back of the wreath, long strands of ribbons were attached so that they hung in long streamers down the back, reaching to the waistline. In later years, hair was parted down the middle, combed to the back, and worked into two long braids and then wound around in a circle at the back of the head.

Something Borrowed, Something Blue

There is an old wedding rhyme that calls for the bride to wear
"Something old, something new,
Something borrowed, something blue."

In all of the research that I have done on Polish weddings of the eighteenth and nineteenth centuries, there was no mention of the bride needing to fulfill this dictum. What I did find was sufficient evidence of the last part of this wedding rhyme which is often forgotten: "And a lucky sixpence in her shoe!" Whether it was a dull copper or a shiny new gold coin, Polish brides have always gone to speak their wedding vows with some money tucked in their shoe, their bodice or within their wedding wreath.

Headpieces for the country bride.

Attendant Dress

The bridal attendants for a country wedding generally wore clothing similar to that of the bride. Most attendants were friends and family from the same village so that their best wear would be almost identical to that worn by the bride. The bride was always easily identified, however, by her hair wreath, the lavishness of her hair ribbons, and of course, by the added sparkle in her eye! Bridesmaids were attired alike in gathered flowered skirts, aprons, white blouses, and embroidered vests with wreaths of flowers containing myrtle and rosemary, or rue in their hair.

Before World War I, the bridesmaids wore long white, rose, green or blue colored skirts and white stockings with white, yellow or black shoes. To complete the outfit the bridesmaids wore lace mittens on their hands. For their hair they wore wreaths with ribbons or bows at the back of their head, to which were attached carnations, roses or myrtle. Also very popular at one time were fans. The bridesmaids hung them at their wrists. At some weddings the bridesmaids carried roses or carnations.

Men's Country Dress

Up until 1900, the regional dress of Cracow was the required dress for a young man getting married and had been for over a hundred years. He often ordered an entire outfit to be made especially for him for his wedding day. The clothes would last him the rest of his life. The Cracow outfit consisted of a hat, a long vest, shirt, pants, belt and boots. I have included all of them here as a point of information. Every bride and groom can decide just how complete they wish the outfit to be. The groom can marry in shirt, pants and boots or the entire outfit including hat, caftan and belt.

Hat

The traditional Cracow hat is called a *rogatywka*. As the name implies, it is a four-cornered hat, usually red in color, with black sheepskin trim around the bottom. Tucked in at one side are two peacock feathers. For something as important as a wedding, the hat would have a fan of peacock feathers across the front with a small bouquet of flowers in the very center.

Caftan or Long Vest

A long blue or black vest called a *kaftan* was another element of men's Cracow dress. It was either plain and unadorned or richly decorated with tassels and embroidery. It was also made with or without a standup collar.

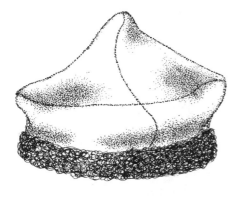

At top: *Rogatywka hat worn by men in eastern regions of Cracow, which is higher than those worn in western region,* **at bottom.**

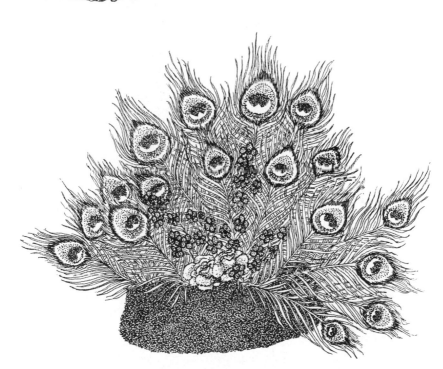

Rogatywka decorated with peacock feathers and flowers for a wedding.

Man's caftan from the Cracow region. Note the initials and date embroidered along the bottom in the side view.

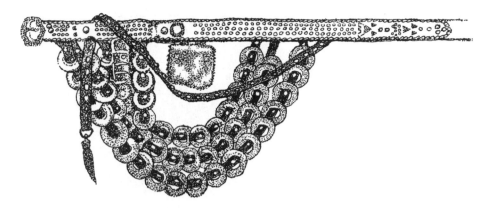

A Cracow belt has a small knife dangling from a thin strip of leather set with studs.

On the more decorative vests, tassels were sewn on both sides from the neck to the waist. The vest had pockets on either side and these, too, were decorated with three to six tassels. There were more tassels in the back at the waist. The colors of the tassels varied. In the southern or northern Krakow regions the tassels were red. In the eastern portions of the region the tassels were green, black or a mix of red, yellow and green.

Alongside the tassels were a row of buttons. The buttons were also strictly decorative since the vest was secured in the front with small hooks and eyes. The vests with red tassels had white buttons. The vests with green tassels had brass buttons. The most decorative vests are said to come from Brzesko. When a young man ordered a vest for his wedding, his initials and the year of his marriage were embroidered at the bottom.

Belt

The vest was held in place by a decorated leather belt. There were two types of belts. The first was a narrow, white leather belt approximately 12 inches wide, which belted with a narrow six-sided brass buckle. The belt was set with brass studs. From the bottom of the belt there hung one, two or three strips of red Moroccan leather hanging in rows, to which were attached round, flat brass disks. These disks were approximately two inches in diameter. All told, there were about fifty disks which jingled and jangled as a man walked or danced. The belt was belted over the vest with the brass disks hanging over the left side.

Also attached to the bottom of the belt was a long, thin strip of leather, set with studs along its length. At the end of the strip, a brass ring held a small folding knife. The leather strip was looped over the belt at the waist

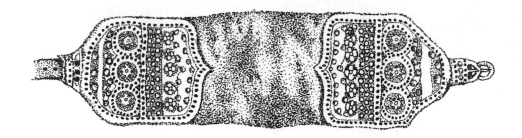

The Cracow belt called opasek was wide and richly tooled.

and allowed to hang down. The earlier belts also had a small leather pouch attached to them, which was used to carry flint.

The second type of leather belt was called an *opasek*. It was worn to the north, south and west of Cracow. This belt was nine to ten inches wide in the center and narrowed at both ends to regular belt width. The center of the belt was left smooth while the sides were richly tooled.

Shirt

The groom wore a white shirt with a small stand-up collar at the neck. The shirt had an opening from the neck to the middle of the chest. Made of homespun linen and later of store-bought muslin, it was embroidered with white thread along the collar, cuffs and center opening. At the neck, a red ribbon was tied into a bow and acted as a tie for special occasions, especially weddings.

Pants

For summer wear, the pants were made of a lightweight cotton/muslin fabric that was slightly gathered at the waist. They were usually white with thin red stripes running lengthwise. Sometimes, instead of red, the stripes were blue. For winter, the pants were made of a heavier fabric such as duck or a cotton/linen blend. The pants were tucked into black knee-high leather boots that were cuffed down at the top—or not—depending upon personal preference.

This regional dress of Cracow began to change after World War I. A young man would marry in dark pants and a suitcoat, with a boutonniere made of myrtle and white ribbons that extended all the way to his knees.

Groomsmen's Dress

The best man and groomsmen were dressed much like the groom, only they wore a hat with a small posy of rose-colored flowers and a short pink ribbon.

Ideas to Borrow from the past:

- After your military wedding, consider making a trip to your local cemetery to place flowers on a tomb dedicated to our fallen soldiers and heroes.

- If you or someone in your family knows the region in Poland that your family came from, consider marrying in a traditional folk costume. Remember that all folk wedding clothes were handmade, and making your own skirts and vests will only add an authentic touch. Or, order a complete costume from someone who deals with Polish costumes. A list of patterns and dealers are listed at the back of the book.

- Make your own wedding dress and a wreath for your hair with white ribbons.

- Make a gift of amber rosary beads to members of the wedding party or a necklace or earrings with amber or coral for the bridesmaids.

Chapter IV

The Wedding Day

The vow of love which thou didst make
I pray that thou wilt ne' er forsake.
Bring it and thy sweet self to me;
No other gift I wish from thee!

> "Song of the Tenth Maiden"
> Jan Kochanowski (1530-1584)

The important day has arrived. All the thought, preparation and effort that has been going on for months will culminate on this day.

If I were to choose which of the Polish wedding customs was the most moving, the most loving, and most impressive, I would have to choose the blessing ceremony. The blessing ceremony is an ancient custom, passed down through the generations. It was still performed in the United States in the early 1950s and 1960s, but has currently disappeared from Polish-American wedding ceremonies altogether. It is possible that readers like you will bring it back into the fold of traditional wedding customs.

Historical Background

The act of parents blessing their children is not a new one. Parents have blessed their offspring since the times of the Old Testament. In Genesis 28:1 we read that "Isaac called Jacob and blessed him." In Genesis 31:55 we find the act: "their father . . . blessed them, blessing each with a blessing suitable to him." Genesis 49:26 also recognizes the importance of such an act with the statement, "the blessings of your father are mighty."

The New Testament also describes parental blessings. In Mark 10:16 "he took them in his arms and blessed them, laying his hands upon them." Further on in Hebrews 11:21 the Bible records that "Jacob blessed each of the sons of Joseph." This importance of receiving parental blessings has continued in Polish life over the centuries, and none was more important than the blessing given on one's wedding day. According to custom, the bride and groom would ask for a blessing from their respective parents before each left for the church to be married. This blessing was seen as even more important than the church ceremony. Children who were blessed by their parents on their wedding day would always do well, prosper steadily, and live a long, successful life together.

Since most marriages took place in the morning, the day's activities began bright and early at the home of the groom. Here, the groomsmen would gather together to help the groom get dressed and be witnesses to the groom's blessing ceremony, along with the groom's immediate family such as aunts, uncles, godparents, brothers and sisters. The musicians hired for the day would also gather at the home of the groom to participate in the blessing ceremony. The musicians could be a four-piece ensemble or a single violin player, depending on availability and the arrangements made by the groom. They played various instruments including the guitar, bass-viol, flute, saxophone, clarinet, drum, harmonica and accordion. The musicians generally had a vast repertoire of selections, both religious and secular, that they would play without sheet music. Almost every aspect of the day was punctuated with either very solemn or lively music. Except for within the church, they played throughout the day.

The Blessing Ceremony at the Home of the Groom

The mother of the groom would prepare a small table that held a candle, crucifix and holy water. She also prepared a handful of her favorite herb, like hyssop or southernwood, tied together tightly at one end to a wooden handle. Some families had or bought a holy water sprinkler. This holy water sprinkler was called a *kropidło*. It was a simpler version of the type used in church, made of a wooden handle with corn husks attached to one end.

The mother and father of the groom stood next to the table while all the assembled guests gathered around. The groom approached his mother and father and generally knelt in front of them. In the presence of the gathered witnesses, the groom asked for a blessing from his parents.

Groom: (kneeling before his parents): "My dearest mother and father. Today I am to be married. Before I go and join my life with another, I want to thank you for all you have done for me, for all of your care and concern over the years. I don't wish to begin this important journey in my life without your blessing."

Mother: "You have our blessing, son. Remember to be good to your wife, cherish her as your helpmate, as the mother of your children." (dipping her herbs in the holy water she sprinkles it on her son and says "In the name of the Father, the Son and Holy Ghost.")

Father: "May you work hard and be a good provider. May you always be faithful to one another." (sprinkles holy water)

During the groom's blessing ceremony the selections played by the musicians were usually *Pobłogosław, Jezu drogi* or *Kto się w opiekę odda Panu Swemu.*

When the blessing at the home of the groom is concluded, everyone who could, went to the home of the bride to witness the blessing ceremony there. Then they would accompany the bride and groom to church.

In the meantime, at the home of the bride, the maid/matron of honor arrived to help with the wedding preparations and especially to help the bride get dressed and await the arrival of her intended.

At the door of the house:

Groom: "I have come to claim my true love, my future wife."

The bride's family allows the groom to enter. Once inside the groom speaks again.

Groom: "Does my future bride send me a sign—a token of her esteem?"

While this dialogue is taking place, the bride is hidden in another room where her bridesmaids are helping her to get dressed. But on hearing his request she sends out her maid/matron of honor with a boutonniere made of rosemary or myrtle tied with a white ribbon.

Maid/Matron of honor: "This is sent to you by your bride (name) who will become your wife today. Take it as a symbol of faith, hope and charity: Faith, that you both will be faithful to one another; Hope, that you both will be hopeful to see each other through difficult times; Charity, that you love one another until death."(Maid/matron of honor pins the boutonniere on the left lapel of the groom).

When the bride is ready, she comes out from where she has been dressing, along with her maid of honor and bridesmaids, for the blessing ceremony and to leave for the church.

The kropidło used for the blessing ceremony at the home of the bride.

The Blessing Ceremony at the Home of the Bride

It is time to go to church. It is time for the young bride to leave the home of her parents. Her husband-to-be has arrived to take her to the church and make her his wife. She will no longer be a single girl under the protection of her parents, but a married woman with responsibilities and children of her own. Just before leaving for the church where the couple will be joined as man and wife, the bride and groom approach her parents. If either parent is missing, someone of equal importance such as a grandparent, godfather, uncle, aunt, guardian or close family friend is substituted. The parents or significant participants are standing near a table where either one or two candles are lit. There is also a small bowl of holy water, a crucifix and, if available, fresh flowers. If flowers are not in season, paper or silk flowers are substituted. A *kropidło* or a clump of herbs tied together is also on hand. Sometimes a special rug or set of pillows was placed on the floor in front of the parents to make the moment a comfortable one. Holding hands, the bride and groom kneel down before them. The bridal party makes a half circle behind the bridal couple while the rest of the friends and family stand behind them. It is the bride who addresses her parents.

Bride: "Dearest mother and father, I am about to leave the home you have given me for so many years. Before I go today, I want to thank you for giving me the precious gift of life, for caring for me, worrying about me and struggling to do your best for me. If I have been ungrateful and

In a blessing ceremony, Paulina and Marcin Krawczyk give the parental blessing to their daughter, Janina, and Józef Junciewicz, April 27, 1957, Buffalo, New York. **Photo courtesy of Annette Junciewicz.**

difficult, if I have hurt you, I ask with all my heart that you forgive me and grant me your blessing."

The parents of the bride hold their hands with palms open over the head of their daughter and her chosen mate while they give their blessing.

Mother of the bride: "We have loved you all the years of your growing up. We forgive and overlook any troubles you may have caused. May you experience a love that is patient and kind and will sustain you through difficulties and hardships. That is my blessing for you. (She takes the *kropidło*, a branch of an herb, or dips her fingers in holy water and sprinkles it on the couple). May you always be faithful to one another. In the name of the Father, the Son and the Holy Ghost."

Father of the bride; "You have my blessing also. May you be strong together. May you always have God before you to direct your actions and your life together. Love one another. (While sprinkling the couple with holy water): May you be blessed by the Father, the Son and the Holy Ghost."

Another set of blessings carry the same sentiments only different words.

Bride: "Dearest parents, we kneel before you on the threshold of married life. Before we leave for church, we would like to receive your blessing."

Mother of the bride: "May the Lord bless you. May He protect you and your new home from harm and danger. Go before the altar and then follow the road of life that has been mapped out for you. (While sprinkling with holy water) In the name of the Father, the Son, and the Holy Ghost."

Father of the bride: "May God guide your steps to the altar. May He also guide all of your steps all the days of your married life. (While sprinkling) May His blessing be with you all the days of your lives."

Another blessing:

Mother: "May God and the people present here today bless you on your new path in life. May you live together in harmony all the days of your lives. As God joins you together, let no one pull you apart."

In the mountain region of southern Poland, the bride's parents often sprinkled the couple with wheat after blessing them with holy water, as a symbol of a "good beginning in their husbandry." The rest of the wedding party also sprinkled them with wheat.

After the blessings are completed, tradition dictates that the musicians play *Serdeczna Matka* or *Witaj Królowo Nieba,* but any other favored church song can be played here. After the music is completed, the bride's father speaks.

Father of the Bride: "Let us say a prayer together for the new pair and those members of the family who have died and cannot be with us today." (Three Our Father's are prayed).

In some households the grandparents also blessed the young couple. If the groom wished to receive his parental blessings at the home of the bride instead of his own, then his mother and father took their turn conducting the blessing after the bride's parents.

The bride and groom rise from their kneeling position and hug and kiss the parents as well as all the friends and family witnessing the event. Immediately after, preparations are made to move on to the church.

Church Ceremony

After the blessings, everyone prepared to leave for the church. The musicians were the first to exit, and posted themselves outside the door to play as everyone left the house. The next to leave were the bride and groom, and as they appeared at the door the musicians struck up a tune while well-wishers who had gathered outside cheered. Sometimes rifles were shot off and whips cracked to acknowledge the importance of the moment.

If the church was nearby, the wedding party walked to church. If not, the traditional method for conveying the entire bridal ensemble, family, and friends to the church was horse-drawn carriages. Among the wealthy, the interior of the carriage or wagon was lined with white velvet or tulle and decorated with myrtle and white ribbons. Two to four horses pulled the conveyance. White or gray horses were preferred, but the reality was that any well-groomed horse was hitched up to the harness. The horse's mane was braided and threaded with flowers and the harnesses polished until they were shiny and bright.

In the snowy mountain regions of Poland, horse drawn sleighs, jingling with hundreds of sleigh bells, were commonly used to take the bride and her entourage to the church.

In southern Poland the lead carriage carried the musicians. The second transported the bride and her bridesmaids. In the third carriage was the groom along with his groomsmen. The rest of the family followed behind in whatever conveyances were at hand, or even walked along behind.

There were numerous variations on this approach. Sometimes the bride and groom rode together in the first carriage with the musicians while the groomsmen rode on horseback alongside as an honor guard. The grooms-men would sometimes shoot rifles and pistols, crack whips, and generally

Wedding party and guests on the way to church in the Rzeszów region, September 1918.

Wedding party on way to church in sleighs and jeeps in mountain region of southern Poland, c. 1960.

make merry the entire route to the church. In other parts of Poland, the bride was escorted by the best man and another groomsman in the first carriage with the groom and the maid of honor following behind. The rest of the guests followed. Another variation was for the bride to be surrounded by her bridesmaids in the carriage, with the groom and grooms-men following along on their horses. The region in which the marriage took place, the time of year, and the conveyances available, dictated how people traveled to the church. Today's modern bride and groom should feel comfortable in deciding how they'd like to travel to church without feeling any qualms about what's right or wrong.

At the church, when everyone descended from the carriages, the musicians took their place by the church entry and played while the wedding party organized themselves into pairs. They continued to play as the bride and groom entered the church and walked down the aisle together, followed by the bridal party and family and friends until everyone was inside the church. When it comes to seating the guests, there have been a number of different approaches. If the church has an altar devoted to the Blessed Virgin Mary, the bride's side of the family was seated on that side. The groom's family was seated on the side of the church that contained the side altar to St. Joseph or the Sacred Heart. Many of these old traditions date back to the times when men and women sat on separate sides of the church—the women on the side of the altar devoted to Mary, Mother of Jesus and the men on the side of the Sacred Heart of Jesus or St. Joseph.

Church Music

When planning your wedding day music, the first thing to consider is where the wedding will take place. If the ceremony will be at a hotel or other location, a piano may be available. If the wedding is being performed in a church, you will need to understand the rules that the church has established regarding music. For example, some churches insist that you use the church organist, or at least pay the organist whether you use him or her or not. Other alternatives to an organist or pianist include a brass quintet, strings, guitar or harp with flute and violin. If you have particular pieces of music in mind, make sure you consider the instrumentation involved.

While your guests are being seated, the background music should be quiet and moving. Popular classics by Mozart, Haydn, and Brahms can provide an appropriate beginning. Also consider pieces by Polish artists such as Chopin, Moniuszko, Szymanowski and Gorecki.

Processional Music

Veni Creator Spiritus has been played as the music of choice for wedding processionals in Poland for centuries. Translated from Latin, it means *Come Greater Spirit*. It first appears in manuscripts dating from the tenth century. In his book, *Memoirs of the Polish Baroque*, Jan Chryzostom Pasek wrote that *Veni Creator* was played as he and his bride approached the altar to be married. The year was 1667. The use of this particular piece of music was true whether the wedding took place in Poland's most magnificent cathedrals or in the humble wooden churches of the countryside.

When Anne of Austria married King Zygmunt II on May 31, 1592 and became Queen of Poland, she walked from the church entrance to the altar to the music of *Te Deum Laudamus (Holy God We Praise Thy Name)*. *Te Deum* has been played at the coronation of Polish queens and marriages of Polish kings for many centuries. It is a chant in praise of God and is generally sung at the end of Matins on Sundays and feast days. It has been played over the centuries as a song of thanksgiving and also as a processional chant.

Music *during* the ceremony varied. In her marriage to King Władysław IV in 1646, Mary Louise de Gonzaga had a children's choir singing. Among the various songs was *Te Deum Laudamus*. Another very simple, but very moving, approach was to have violin solos performed during various portions of the service. If you want to do some research before you select the music for your ceremony, check your local libraries or music stores.

In older times, the groomsmen and bridesmaids of Poland entered the church first and made an arch with their hands, through which the bride and groom passed on their way to the altar. Then each pair of attendants followed behind them through the arch until only one remained and then that last pair joined hands and followed everyone else down the aisle.

The bride and groom knelt in the center of the sanctuary, while the bridesmaids and groomsmen paired off behind them to the left and right with the youngest attendants behind the bride and groom. (See diagram below) As a special recognition, a white cloth was placed under the couple's feet.

The altar was lit with numerous candles and lavishly decorated with flowers from the gardens of family and friends. The priest generally said the Mass first and then the marriage vows were exchanged.

The exchange of the marriage vows is the essence, the very heart, of all the other activities that are taking place on this important day. Many couples choose to write their own vows. Others choose to read the words of their favorite writers or poets. Notes still extant from 1514 in the city of Cracow offer the text of the line of questioning at the time of the exchange of wedding vows. They are similar to the vows couples take today. The priest asked the names of the individuals kneeling before him and then began his line of questioning.

Priest: According to the holy rights of the church, I ask you (name) and you (name), are you here to enter into the state of marriage?

After receiving their affirmative responses, he gave them a brief homily on the sanctity of marriage and then continued his questioning.

Priest: I ask you (name of groom), have you ever married another, other than the one that stands before you?

He asks the same question of the bride. After hearing her response, the priest again turned to the groom.

Priest: Do you see (name of bride) who kneels here beside you in a healthy state due to the grace of God? If later by some misfortune, she is no longer healthy, will you remain faithful?

He repeats the same question for the bride to answer. Receiving an affirmative response, he joins their hands together and asks the groom to repeat after him:

Priest: I, (name) take you (name) for my lawfully wedded wife and marry you holding sacred the sacrament of marriage until the time of my death so help me God, the Blessed Mother and all the saints.

The bride repeats the same vow.

After the wedding ceremony was completed, it was time for the newly married couple to face the congregation and exit the church as man and wife. In Polish wedding tradition, there is one more rite or act that precedes this very joyous and triumphant exit from the church. It consisted of the newly married young woman visiting the altar of the Blessed Virgin Mary.

Just before the congregation stood to greet the couple at the end of the service, the organist began playing the prelude to *Ave Maria*. On hearing these beginning notes the bride stood and received the bouquet of flowers from her maid of honor that had been prepared for this moment. The bouquet was generally of white lilies, the acknowledged symbol of the Blessed Virgin Mary in Christian liturgy. She slowly walked to the altar where she placed the bouquet, and then knelt at the foot of the altar and prayed with bowed head. During this solemn moment the bride paid homage to the Patroness of Poland, prayed for health for herself and her new husband and vowed to be a good mother to her future children. At the conclusion of the music, the bride rose and returned to her husband's side, holding out her hand to him. He grasped it, and together they faced the congregation and began making their way out of the church.

Recessional

The bride and groom proceed down the aisle, followed by the attendants in pairs. In some Polish weddings there were variations on this approach. When the bride and groom faced the congregation to walk down the aisle as a married couple, the bridesmaids and groomsmen lined up across from each other forming a special honor guard as the bride and groom left the altar area. The maid of honor and best man stood closest to the bride and groom. After the bride and groom passed through this honor guard, the maid of honor and best man would pair off and walk through the honor guard also and down the central aisle past the congregation, followed by the next couple, and the next until the last remaining couple walked down the aisle.

The music for the recessional should be joyous, and many couples have chosen very unique pieces and instruments to capture the moment forever—an entire chorus singing a joyful song or the strong notes of a trio of trumpets. It should echo the joy in the hearts of the bride and groom. Unknown to many is the fact that Poland has a very old history of playing bagpipes. This is especially true in the Śląsk region of Poland where bagpipes were made of goat or sheepskin. Mikołaj Rej, one of Poland's oldest chroniclers, wrote that many of the nobles and gentry entertained themselves and their friends with the music of bagpipes. Many Polish proverbs such as *A Weselejby było, kiedyby byty dudy* testify to the merriment added to any festivity by the music of bagpipes. The proverb states "It would be merrier, if only we had bagpipes." So, why not bagpipes?

As the couple exited from church, they were showered with wheat, rye or oat grains as a symbol that they may always have plenty, especially bread, to eat. At the weddings of nobles and monarchs, it was customary to throw coins at the people who had gathered to witness the emergence of the wedded couple from the church. Coins, with the likeness of the king, were newly minted for the occasion.

Karolina Kozłowska and Wawr-zyniel Wieczorek, St. Stanislaus Kostka Church, Niagara Falls, NY, January 28, 1918.

Karolina Kozłowska Wieczorek, January 28, 1918.

Family wedding photo of Karolina Kozłowska and Wawrzyniec Wieczorek, Niagara Falls, January 28, 1918.
All photos this page courtesy of Brian Stanish and Mrs. Emily Stanish.

Among many prosperous families living in Warsaw, there was a custom of arranging for the newly married couple to take a drive through the loveliest parts of the city. There was such a wedding route in Łazienki Park in Warsaw, as well as near the palace of Wilanów. The couple rode in a specially arranged black carriage with seats lined in white satin. Part of the ritual of the ride was to stop along the way at a photography studio and have their picture taken. This portrait was then hung over their marriage bed.

Because having a photograph taken was expensive in the early years of photography, only the most momentous occasions were recorded for posterity. Among these occasions were weddings, when families from all around the country gathered together to witness and celebrate the marriage of a niece or cousin.

Ideas to borrow from the past

- If the notion of having the groom see the bride before the church ceremony is too different to accept for either bride or groom, then the blessing ceremony could take place in the church before the beginning of the service, just as the bride is delivered to the groom at the altar. This would be in keeping with the tradition, and still be witnessed by those who came to celebrate the important event. It can be a very lovely moment for all present. Discuss this with your priest/minister or whoever is presiding at the ceremony.

- The blessing ceremony offered here is from text used in Poland, but each bride, groom and parents can formulate their personal blessings.

- Use wheat or oats to throw at the bride and groom when coming out of church instead of birdseed or rose petals.

- If you have access to, and do not live not too far away from where your wedding ceremony is going to be held, try hiring a traditional horse and carriage. It's a piece of history that today's bridal couple can live and experience due to the popularity of horse-drawn vehicles throughout the United States. Check for a sleigh and carriage leasing business in your state by writing to the Carriage Association of America, listed in the Sources at the back of the book. However, if that isn't feasible use hired limousines, taxis or cars. They are being used even in Poland today.

- If it is in keeping with your faith and philosophy, have a separate bouquet made and take it to the altar of the Blessed Virgin Mary.

- According to Polish custom, the groom hired and paid for the band.
- The groom or best man always gave each of the altar boys an envelope with a special tip for helping serve the Mass.

Chapter V

The Wedding Reception

Old Polish Wedding Toast

To the health of the groom
May he live a long life!

To the health of the bride
May she be generous in sharing her pillow!

To the bridesmaids
Who refuse to share their pillows!

Drink, drink until there's nothing left
And may you in the Lord's blessings be kept!

*F*ollowing the church ceremony, guests headed for the home where the wedding reception was to be held. Oftentimes this was at the home of the bride or even at a neighbor's house. It was also very common to hold receptions at a public inn where there were plenty of tables to accommodate all the guests. This was especially true by the second half of the nineteenth century.

Greetings with Bread and Salt

One of the very important old Polish rituals associated with the arrival of the guests at a wedding was greeting them with a plate of rye bread sprinkled with salt. This was very traditional among all classes of people in Poland and was not limited to weddings. When expecting guests for any special occasion, the housewife prepared bread and salt and offered it to anyone entering within. The most common interpretation behind offering guests these two items dates back to antiquity when both these items were considered among the most basic and essential of foodstuffs. The purpose of greeting with bread and salt was to assure the young couple fertility and plenty in their husbandry. Good Polish hospitality dictated (and still does) that you offer your guests the best that your home can provide. Bread was revered as sacred. It was considered the staff of life, the highest gift from God. Even crumbs on a table were swept into an apron and given to the birds or chickens. Salt, on the other hand, was essential for the preservation of food. In ancient beliefs salt also had the power to cleanse and to protect. Symbolically, both these items represent the bitterness of life as well as the goodness.

Usually it was the role of the parents to meet each entering guest at the door with a plate covered with one's best linen cloth containing small pieces of bread sprinkled with a tiny amount of salt. In very ancient times the plate was actually the top of a dough bin which was used for making the very bread that was being offered to the guests. In some parts of Poland, such as Rzeszów, the wedding guests were greeted with bread, salt and sugar. In Polish-American customs, the musicians played the *Wedding March*.

To each arriving guest, the mother and father of the bride would offer a piece of bread and salt with simple words of welcome:

"We greet you and invite you to our home on this joyous occasion with this bread and salt."

When the bride and groom returned from the photographer, they also were greeted by the bride's parents with bread and salt. They crossed over the threshold and entered the room where the mother of the bride was waiting for them. In Śląsk, the bride and groom were expected to sing a church hymn called *U Drzwi Twoich* (*At Your Door*) before crossing the threshold to where her parents waited for the couple. The words reveal that they stand before (God's) door waiting for His Mercy and recognize that God is hidden in the bread. As the couple cross the threshold, the mother of the bride speaks.

102

Mother of the bride: "When God created the world He first created bread, water and salt for man to live. You must eat this bread and salt so that you may never experience lack of them in your life."

Another greeting that accompanied the offering of bread and salt to the bride and groom:

Mother of the bride: "We greet you with this bread and salt that you may never know hunger and that your home should always be host to friendship and plenty."

Bride: "We thank you with all of our heart."

Groom: "We will both work hard to earn our daily bread."

Father of the bride(to the groom): "I accept you (_____)in my home not as a son-in-law but as my own son."

Groom: "Thank you. I am happy to have you as my father."

In some parts of Poland, the groom took the bread, sprinkled salt on it, then broke off a piece and shared it with his new wife.

The bride's father then sprinkled them with oats.

In Leżajsk, also in the Rzeszów region, the bride and groom were greeted with bread, salt and a sweet wine. All three symbolized the goodness and bitterness of life.

Ideas to Borrow from the Past:

* Most of today's wedding photographs are made on the spot at the wedding, but there is something very old fashioned in making a special trip to a photographer for a wedding portrait. Have it done in black and white or sepia tone. These photographs are more in keeping with wedding photographs of the past.

Decorations

There is no limit to what can be done to transform a room into a reception hall. The bridal pair can pick almost any combination of flowers, linen and centerpieces to give the room the look that they're seeking. There are a few historical aspects about Polish dining customs, however, that should be considered.

From time immemorial, the table has brought people together to break bread. In Polish homes, the table is at the crux of all gatherings and is taken very seriously. Polish historians remind us that all classes of people covered their tables with linen. Among the rich and famous, the tables were covered with costly tablecloths that were beautifully embroidered and sometimes studded with gems. Even in less well-to-do homes, the inventories of table linens were large and varied. Some were used for dinner and other colored ones for serving coffee and desserts. Even among the poorer classes, a cloth made of homespun linen was placed on the table when guests were expected. While traveling through Poland in 1635-1636, the French diplomat, Charles Ogier noted in his travel diary that at a reception at the home of the powerful and influential Stanisław Lubomirski, a "tablecloth artistically embroidered heightened the effect of the china."

The references to the tablecloth are not casual comments. Its function was to join people together at the table. If there was among the diners someone with a very bad name or tarnished reputation, or someone who had conducted himself with dishonor, the tablecloth was cut in front of him as a sign that he sits and eats alone. This is a very old custom dating earlier than the sixteenth century because Mikołaj Rej (1505-1569), the first poet to describe Polish life in the Polish language, wrote of it as inherited from our Polish forefathers. To remind someone that the tablecloth was at one time cut in front of their ancestor was considered the greatest of insults.

Polish historians also note that for weddings the tables were covered with white tablecloths and decorated with greenery. The table could be decorated with rue and clusters of red berries from viburnum *(Viburnum opulus),* which is generally available in late August and early September. The tables were often decorated with wild flowers gathered from the countryside. According to one historian, "these were not tall bouquets but a not too wide band of multicolored petals running along the center of the table." Sometimes the wedding hall or reception room was decorated with ribbons and branches of spruce and fir. This would work especially well for a winter wedding. On the tables, candles or hurricane lamps were also used as centerpieces.

The Wedding Menu

Many of today's caterers report that couples are paying greater attention to selecting appropriately planned menus that complement the spirit of the wedding reception. The wedding menu is determined by the type of wedding you are having. If you are planning a medieval Christmas wedding, rich with velvet and brocades, the wedding meal might consist of a giant feast with authentic fare such as roast pork, turkey drumsticks and hearty stews. The table should reflect the abundance of the period with baskets of bread and rolls, platters of roasted meats and vegetables, plenty of cheese and fruit and a huge, ornate wedding cake that captures the spirit of the times.

If you are opting for something Victorian, then you are likely to hold a "wedding breakfast." This is usually held at lunch time and consists of a sumptuous repast served as a buffet or a sit-down meal. Table settings will include lace tablecloths, silver and fine china with very carefully selected flower arrangements. You would serve a red wine or champagne and have a traditional layered wedding cake. A smaller wedding on a limited budget can still be a lovely affair with the addition of a special dessert, an imported wine, or a special coffee.

Whether you plan a Victorian tea, a military wedding, an Easter time wedding or a simple Polish country wedding, it is important to take inspiration from the past rather than try to re-create it down to the last detail. Wedding receptions can be as lavish or as simple as one desires or can afford. Doing something special, such as serving an imported wine or offering guests special after-dinner drinks of Polish liqueurs, cordials or brandy served from liqueur carts, can give your reception a special touch of class. The rule of Polish hospitality is to offer guests the best that one can afford.

Historical Perspective

To study old Polish cuisine is to know that it had a very distinct character that combined the best of its own national dishes with the best of other nations. Lying in the heart of Europe, Poland had excellent soil for growing rye and wheat as well as barley and buckwheat. In its early prime, Poland ranked as one of Europe's top exporters of grain. Buckwheat groats, barley, millet, rye and wheat were floated on barges on the Wisła River to Gdańsk, and then shipped to all parts of Europe. The people of Poland enjoyed numerous dishes made of cereals and grains. Kasha, made from buckwheat groats, was prepared and enjoyed in the homes of the rich and the poor. Wheat and rye flours were used for an infinite variety of dumplings, breads, cakes and pastries.

In its earliest years, Polish cuisine depended heavily on its own indigenous herbs and spices to flavor food, such as anise, caraway and horseradish. Foods were very sharp tasting and tended to be sour and salty, with generous use of garlic, onion, pickles, fermented cabbage and black bread. Mushrooms were found on the tables of both the privileged and the humble cottager. Entire families headed out to the forests and meadows after a summer or autumn rain to spend the day mushroom hunting. There were numerous types of mushrooms. Some, like orange and birch boletes, were more suitable for drying. The mushrooms were strung on a string or pickled in vinegar. Dried and marinated mushrooms were also used to enhance the flavor of foods. They were used to make mushroom soup, add flavoring and depth to vegetables, sauces and meats, and used as appetizers.

Increased contact with the East brought spice traders, and Poland fell in love with seasonings and spices. Pepper, saffron, cloves, mustard seeds, and ginger all found a permanent home in Polish kitchens as did raisins, pine nuts, almonds, lemons, olives, figs and nuts.

The food item that gained the most attention on Polish tables was meat. Except for the homes of the very wealthy and upper classes, meat was not part of everyday meals for most of the inhabitants of Poland. Meat appeared on the table for very special occasions, and weddings, of course, were one of those special times. Meat became the centerpiece of any major Polish gathering. Pork prepared as sausages was a perennial favorite. Other meat dishes included goose, veal, chicken, turkey, and capons.

For a long time lamb was considered an inferior cut of meat, but it became popular under Polish King Stanisław Poniatowski (1764-1795), who was a great lover of lamb. During his reign, he held special dinner parties which became known in history as the "Thursday dinners." The king invited educators, artists, writers and poets to talk and eat. Lamb prepared with garlic was served frequently at these dinners, and it soon became a specialty item at Polish dinner tables.

Beef was smoked or prepared in aspic. Vast tracts of forests provided unlimited access to wild game, including deer, quail, partridge, duck and grouse. Writing about Polish banquets held in the eighteenth century, chroniclers describe: "Two servants carried in one enormous platter because one could not carry it alone. At the bottom of the platter were the sides of oxen. On top of that were quarters of veal, then lamb, turkey, goose, capons, chickens, quail, snipe and so on and so on, gradually getting smaller."

Fish was an item that was frequently served to guests. Polish chefs were noted for their ability to prepare fish. Guillame Beauplan, a French engineer and cartographer who spent time in Poland and generally did not have too many favorable things to say about Polish cooking, wrote: "There is something in which Poles surpass us and that is regarding fish. They do miraculous things with it...they prepare it so well and give it such excellent taste that it will awaken the appetite of even the most surfeit individual.

They surpass all other nations and it is not only my taste or my opinion but the belief of all Frenchmen and other foreigners who have been there."

One of the most popular fishes was herring. It used to serve as a main staple during fast days, but continues to be one of the most popular of Polish appetizers. Sturgeon and salmon from the Wisła were considered luxury items. Pike, sterlet (a small sturgeon found in the Caspian Sea), trout, eel and carp were among other species of fish that were enjoyed in Poland. The writings of other foreigners and dignitaries concurred with that of Beauplan. They indicated that "in the kitchen one wished for a Polish chef to prepare the fish and a French chef to prepare the pâté."

Added to the meat and fish were local vegetables. The most popular was cabbage, both sweet and fermented, as well as carrots, turnips, parsnips and beets. Potatoes, served in numerous ways, were a national favorite.

The meals were generally concluded with sweets. Among the rich, large silver platters engraved with the family crest or monogram were loaded with a variety of candied fruits. Cherries, currants, gooseberries, plums, and pears, as well as almonds and walnuts were covered with white sugar and anise. There were also fresh fruits, sponge cakes, tortes and honey cakes. Compotes made of fresh or dried fruits were a favorite among rich and poor alike.

Like many other cuisines of the world, Polish cooking was influenced by its neighbors. Poland has assimilated the dishes of almost every country—Russia, Turkey, Sweden, Germany, France, Italy and Spain. Marriages with men and women from other countries introduced a variety of foodstuffs and dishes to Poland. As a result, to sit down to eat at a Polish table was to find the best of Polish cuisine, as well as the best of the rest of the world. The French fashion of stuffing game birds and meats with bread and herbs became fashionable at the homes of the rich trendsetters. Bouillons, delicately flavored soups, and the use of wine and lemons instead of vinegar in food preparation, began to influence Polish cooking.

The English way of cooking also became fashionable in Poland. William Cox, an Englishman visiting Poland in 1778 wrote in his *Travels through Poland* that he was served an English "cold collation" while visiting the fabulously wealthy Czartoryski family in Powązka. He wrote: "We sat down to a wide array of delicacies with costly wines and the rarest of fruit." "English style" breakfasts also became *a la mode* with hunks of roast beef, pudding and drinks such as arrack, rum, port and beer being served.

The history of Polish hospitality is, of course, legendary. Like Mr. Cox's account, numerous literary sources, memoirs and chronicles of foreigners who visited Poland, noted not only the distinct character, originality and variety of Polish cooking, but documented the hospitality of the country's inhabitants. The meaning of Polish hospitality rings clear in the proverb "A guest in the house is God in the house." Whether it be the home of the rich and well-known, or the poor and humble, each guest was treated as a valuable and welcome addition to the table, and served "*czem chata bogata*," i.e., the very best that the house could afford. In order to make the guest feel comfortable and at home, the rules of Polish hospitality also demanded that the menu offer foods that were familiar to the guest.

In the seventeenth century, the Papal nuncio Onorio Visconti wrote to his friends, detailing the foods he had been served at receptions given in his honor in Poland. A mixture of Polish and Italian dishes were served, including pâté, stuffed capons, partridges, fowl, pigeon, and salami. A variety of vegetables included salads and Spanish olives. Among the traditional Polish dishes served were sauerkraut, lobster, snail, and imported delicacies such as grapes, dates, sweetened almonds, raisins, nuts and figs.

Wedding feasts were accounted to be the grandest of family celebrations, and many efforts were made to offer the best that the house could afford and to make guests feel welcome and at home.

When Felicjan Potocki led the daughter of Jerzy Lubomirski to the altar in 1681, the match united two of the foremost families of Poland. The groom's father was Field Marshal of the Polish Crown, the equivalent to commander-in-chief of Poland's armed forces. Among the guests were fifteen hundred dignitaries and nobles, as well as the Field Marshal's own private army, consisting of 1200 soldiers and mercenaries from other lands. To say that the reception was an enormous affair is to make an understatement. Sixty oxen were killed, along with 300 calves, 120 piglets, 500 lambs, 6,000 capons, 8,000 chickens, 2,000 turkeys, 1,500 ducks and 500 geese. The slaughter didn't end there. From the forests and game preserves came twenty-four stags, forty-five deer, 2,000 grouse hens, 1,000 wild geese, 500 wild ducks, 300 garganey (a small fresh water European duck) and twelve bustard (another European game bird.)

The guests were also treated to many varieties of fish. Pike, carp, cod, flounder, lamprey and salmon all graced the tables. Vegetables, fruits, sweets and desserts were served, as well as barrels of mead and hundreds of bottles of Hungarian wines. Everything was prepared in astronomical quantities by four master chefs, seventy-five cooks, four French bakers, and six pastry chefs. Six hundred servants were designated to carry out the platters and attend to the guests.

The wedding feast of King Władysław, son of Zygmunt III, with Cecylia Renata in 1637, was an even more opulent affair. Since this was the marriage of a king to an Austrian princess, the wedding menu was staggering. Two hundred oxen were slaughtered to provide beef. Forty thousand chickens and twenty thousand geese were killed. There were also various kinds of wild game and fish courses, all in grander numbers and more ostentatiously presented and served.

Describing the wedding feast of Bona Sforza, Giuliano Passero, a countryman to Bona Sforza, began his account by writing "It was made certain that the guests lacked for nothing." Among the guests were individuals from Poland and from Italy, and efforts were made to please the palate of all who attended. Giuliano Passero was such a careful observer of the proceedings that he even documented the order in which the food was served! Included in his list were: a meat aspic with lettuce; meat in a white sauce with mustard; roasted pigeons, followed by roasted beef with vinegar dressing; partridge with sour apples and a preserve of figs; French pastries with cheese; wild boar fixed in the Hungarian manner; pâté; and stuffed peacock. There was a brief respite and then more food: "game with noodles, roasted pheasant and a cheese cake baked the Spanish way." The meal was concluded with "an ancient Neapolitan dish made of a delicate dough covered with sugar. This was served with a white wine heated with honey and spices."

Opulent wedding feasts were the norm even among rich city merchants and burghers. Charles Ogier, traveling through Poland, was invited to the wedding feast of a rich Polish merchant in Gdansk. In his memoirs he recalls that the wedding feast alone lasted from 2 P.M. to 7 P.M.

Even country weddings called for a lamb, cow or calf to be slaughtered, and a fresh keg of beer brewed. In her memoirs, a country woman in 1644 documented that for her stepdaughter's wedding she "slaughtered a cow, prepared a keg of beer and three jugs of vodka."

According to old Polish traditions, the wedding feast should have at least ten different items on the menu.

Wedding Day Spirits

For some brides and grooms, a minimal amount of thought goes into the liquor and beverage selection for their reception. Yet stocking a bar for a wedding is not an easy task. You need to serve the preferences of a wide range of age groups, and people with different tastes and lifestyles. You may want to explore the possibility of selecting a few special drinks for your reception.

Beer, made of wheat, oats and barley, was one of the most common drinks of Europe, including Poland, for many centuries. An old legend rumors that one of the earliest Piasts (first rulers of Poland during the eleventh century) named Konrad, son of Prince Glogowski, obtained a very prestigious position in the church in the city of Salzburg. By the time he arrived in Austria he had consumed the last barrel of beer that he had brought along with him on his long trip. On learning that the city failed to have the particular brand of beer he customarily drank, he promptly resigned his new post and returned home!

Poland lays claim to some of the finest breweries in the world, with many of its brews imported into the United States. These include a brand called Zywiec.

Another common drink was mead. This was a drink made of fermented honey and water. The weaker meads took the place of beer. A variety of mead was made into fruit cordials from raspberries and cherries, based on a one-to-one proportion with honey.

In the seventeenth century, wine began appearing on Polish tables with greater frequency. This does not mean that wine was unknown in Poland until that time. Indeed, wine was served in Poland from medieval times. Grape wine was being produced in the thirteenth and fourteenth centuries on the left bank of the Wisła River, between Sandomierz and Cracow. The wine was intended for priests saying Mass, or for the courts of kings and nobles. Even at the beginning of the fifteenth century, wine was considered a luxury item, and drunk only on high holidays and during special events. In the late sixteenth century and beginning of the seventeenth, with the increased wealth of the upper classes who could afford to import wine in large quantities from other countries, drinking wine became more common in Poland. The practice gradually became more widespread and reached even the middle classes. All types of wines—French, Spanish, Dutch, Hungarian and Italian—found favor in Poland. So did madeira, tokay, burgandy, bordeaux and champagne. Hungarian wine was one of the most costly luxury items of the eighteenth century. It was considered to be the best of all wines, and was very expensive. A French chronicler once stated this about a Polish wedding: "During a wedding one drinks only Hungarian wine while making numerous toasts to the bride and groom amidst the blaring of trumpets and drums. This goes on sometimes till dawn."

Hungarian wines, and later on French wines, were among Poland's most expensive imports. They ranked in importance with spices from the Far East, which were used to flavor meats and baked goods. Hungarian, French, Spanish and German wines flowed uninterrupted in the homes of the wealthy. Wine was served in enormous goblets. Champagne was consumed like cider.

As Poland was importing wines, it was exporting its own spirits as well. When Pablo Picasso was once asked to name the three most important new features of post-war French culture, he said, "Modern jazz, Bridgette Bardot and Polish vodka." The artist was referring to the many distinctive Polish vodkas that have become famous worldwide.

The name "vodka" is derived from the Russian phrase *zhizennia voda*, meaning *water of life*. Initially, it was called *okowita* from the Latin *aqua vitae*, also meaning *water of life*. The Russians maintain that vodka was invented in their country in the fourteenth century, and that the secret of making it spread from Russia to Finland to Poland. At first, vodka in Poland was made by monks and apothecaries and used medicinally. In 1546, King Jan Olbracht passed a law allowing every citizen to make and sell spirits. The result was that every family prepared its own vodkas and often flavored them with fruits, roots, seeds and herbs. Polish vodkas featured the taste of berries, like cherry, or offered the tang of green walnuts. The flavors of anise, caraway, pokeberry, cinnamon, wormwood, mulberry, and clove were also added to the vodka. All of the larger manor houses had their own distilleries, distilling the vodka three different times into different strengths, all done under the watchful eye of the housewife. Traditionally, a vodka was bottled at the birth of a daughter and consumed at her wedding feast.

By the sixteenth century, vodka was being made and consumed in ever increasing numbers. One of the oldest names in Polish vodkas, dating back to 1601, was founded by the Zamoyski family. The major center for vodka production was Poznań, which had forty-nine distilleries even in the sixteenth century.

In the seventeenth and eighteenth centuries vodka from Gdansk was very popular. The most favored one was called *Goldwasser*. The recipe for it was a carefully guarded secret. All that was known was that it was loaded with anise, was very sweet and contained flakes of gold. There were other brands of Polish vodka that were also held in high regard. *Jałowcówka* was produced from juniper berries. *Żubrówka*, a vodka whose name comes from a grass floating in the bottle, is very popular in Poland. In botanical terms, the grass is *Hierochloe odorata*, and grows wild in moist places in most of Eastern Europe and the British Isles. It adds a softness and mildly sweet vanilla taste to the vodka. It is a familiar vodka to Poles, Russians and Czechs, and growing in popularity in the United States. *Wyborowa*, a name brand of 80 proof vodka imported from Poland and made from rye, is also available in the United States. Other brands of Polish vodka available in the United States are 100 proof *Luksusowa* and 80 proof *Belvedere*. The newest vodka imported from Poland is *Chopin Vodka*. It is made from Stobrawa potatoes, which are cultivated and harvested in the Siedlice region of Poland.

Many Polish drinking customs are tied to vodka. As noted by a writer from the second half of the seventeenth century "here in Poland we use vodka for everything...for sleep, for itching, for worries, for appetite, for appearance and forwardness...it is ostensibly a medicine that one cannot do without, and is used to seal agreements, sales, reconciliations and courtships." The writer's earlier comments about vodka's medicinal qualities are significant. At one time in Poland, vodka was seen as highly medicinal, especially for stomach ailments. A tiny glass was offered to a guest with the words *"daj wam Bóg zdrowie"* i.e. God grant you health. From there it is just a small step towards the Polish drinking toast *"Na Zdrowie!"* (To your health!)

Another group of spirits that gained tremendous popularity in Poland were cordials and liqueurs. The word "liqueur" comes to us from Latin and means "to melt" or "dissolve." That describes figuratively what happens when a flavoring substance comes into contact with a neutral alcohol. The essence of the plant, herb, seed or fruit dissolves into the alcohol, giving it flavor, aroma and sometimes color, which in turn, becomes the character of the alcohol. Liqueurs are luscious sweet drinks that capture the essence of fruits, berries, flowers, herbs, spices and nuts. In the United States, a drink must have at least 22% sugar to qualify as a liqueur or cordial. Many, however, have a lot more. Liqueurs (a word used interchangeably with cordial) have been consumed from the times of the Greeks, but it was during the Middle Ages that they became widely popular. Monks were distilling them within the confines of the monastery stillroom and dispensing them as life-restoring remedies. As the centuries passed and life became more modern, every noble had a small still. Each lady of the manor took pride in her own special recipes, trying to outdo her rivals with new and fascinating flavors. Spices and fruits from the New World, such as pineapple and oranges, were converted into digestive liqueurs and offerings of domestic hospitality. No matter what time of day, guests were greeted with a small glass of sweet liqueur. In flavors of pineapple, mint, oranges and cherries, these drinks were also a favorite at any social gathering. Of great popularity is the honeyed liqueur called *Krupnik*. A favorite cherry liqueur made in Poland is *Wiśniówka*.

One final comment about drinks and drinking customs in Poland. It is interesting to note that those abstaining from drinking were considered to have had a poor upbringing. Giulio Ruggieri, the papal nuncio residing in Poland during the years 1566-1568, noted that "sobriety is considered rude and sometimes a sign of a sly, underhanded character."

Cocktail Reception with Appetizers

In Poland, appetizers are called *zakąski*, meaning "small bites." The custom of serving them is a very old one, probably originating among the aristocracy on their country estates. With bad roads, travel was often long and difficult. If people were traveling in the winter, it was also dangerous and cold. Guests would arrive at any time of the day or night, without advance warning, and were generally famished. The *zakąski* took the edge off their hunger while a meal could be prepared. These small bites of food were items found in the larder or pantry that had been put down over the summer and fall season. These generally included pickles and relishes, pickled eggs and vegetables, smoked meats and sausages, pâtés put down in thick crocks and sealed with fat to prevent spoiling. There were thick, hearty breads baked in wood ovens.

Appetizers could be served cold or hot. Cold appetizers range from simple, easily prepared and readily available items such a hard-cooked eggs in various guises, assorted cold cuts, and pâtés. Hot appetizers need to be cooked in advance and heated just before serving. Both types of appetizers are found in traditional menus. It would be interesting to plan a Polish appetizer table for your wedding, but there is also excitement and interest in putting together a mix-and-match menu from around the world. Cheese in its many forms was central to the Polish wedding menu. Goat cheese, currently enjoying a revival in America, was at one time a staple of Polish cuisine. Both the humble cottager and the powerful lords of the manor kept goats to supply milk that would be made into cheese. *Pierogi*, dumplings filled with meat, cheese, and sauerkraut, can also be served. The pierogi can be made into larger, more filling hôrs d'ouvres or small and dainty ones. They make perfect little appetizers that always seem to garner rave reviews. Nuts, raisins and figs were already being imported into Poland in great quantities in the eighteenth century and were served at all important gatherings.

Sample Menu:

Appetizer Table #1
Grilled Sausage with Sweet Mustard and Hot Horseradish
Herring Platter (Rolled Marinated, Wine Sauce, Sour Cream Sauce)
Thinly Sliced Smoked Ham
Goat Cheese with Dill Canapés
Shrimp and Dill Canapés
Chicken Liver Pâté
Marinated Mushrooms
Beet Relish
Mushroom Stuffed Eggs
Cornichons(French Sour Gerkins)
Black Cherry Crepes
Thinly Sliced Black Bread, Rye and Pumpernickel
Iced Clear Vodka
Iced Flavored Vodka
Krupnik

Appetizer Table #2
Caviar
Smoked Salmon Canapés
Goose Liver Pâté
Thinly Sliced Smoked Turkey
Sliced Roast Beef
Pickled Beets and Onions
Marinated Mushrooms
Baskets of Assorted Breads
Iced Clear Vodka
Iced Flavored Vodka
Krupnik

Ideas to Borrow From the Past:

- To add more of a Polish flavor to your wedding reception, have tiny glasses available and serve Polish vodka along with the hôrs d'ouvres. Be sure to chill the vodka in the freezer. Its high alcohol content will keep it from turning to ice but it will be ice cold and entirely refreshing. Have someone offer a toast to the bridal couple and consume it in the old traditional style—tossed back in one fiery gulp.

The Buffet

It is not a big budget that makes the menu an important part of the reception, but rather, taste and presentation. Flowers, fine linen, and gleaming serving pieces make all the difference in a successful buffet table. A buffet or family-style menu is very popular and can be done tastefully.

Buffet #1
Country Sausage
Breaded Pork Chops
Steak Roll-ups with Bread Stuffing
Baked Chicken
Broiled New Potatoes
Cauliflower with Green Herbed Crumb Topping
Sweet and Sour Cabbage
Pickled Mushrooms

Buffet #2
Country Ham
Roast Beef with Mushrooms
Sauerkraut with Polish Sausage
Stuffed Cabbage Rolls
Country Style Potatoes
Pierogi with Potato and Cheese
Broccoli and Cauliflower Casserole
Cucumbers in Sour Cream
Fresh Fruit Compote
Baskets of Rolls and Black Bread

Wedding Breakfast Buffet
Country Ham
Grilled Country Sausages
Scrambled Eggs Florentine
Potato Pancakes with Applesauce
Crepes with Ligonberry Jam
Blintz with Cheese
Toasted English Muffins
Sunflower Seed Bread/Fresh Rolls
Almond Pastry

The Wedding Dinner

Traditionally, the first course in any Polish meal, either for a wedding, dinner party, or family supper was soup. In the winter, it was a hot soup. Beet, barley, chicken and cabbage soups are true Polish soups. Barley with beef and pea soup, cooked with smoked bacon and topped with croutons, was hearty fare that delighted guests. In the summer, cold soups called a *chłodnik* were very popular. In the times when Lithuania and Poland were united as one country, a cold soup was made from chopped beet greens and thinly sliced vegetables such as beets, cucumbers, or radishes and served with sour cream. Fruit soups were also a favorite in the summertime, especially cold blueberry or strawberry soup. In a Polish country wedding, the dishes served were simple but hearty fare, delivered on the best plates or pottery owned by the family. Generous quantities of beer or vodka were offered to the guests. The following are just a few suggestions for menus that may be appropriate for sit-down dinners.

Wedding Dinner #1

Potato, Leek and Parsley Soup
and/or
Marinated Vegetable Salad
Beef Tenderloin with Herbed Cream Sauce
Wild Rice with Barley and Mushrooms
Asparagus with Lemon Butter

Wedding Dinner #2

Chicken Soup with Egg Noodles
and/or
Dilled Cucumber Salad
Roast Duck with Blackberry Sauce
Bulgar Wheat Pilaf
Red Cabbage

Wedding Dinner #3

Beet Soup with Mushroom Dumplings
and/or

Fresh Green Salad
Roasted Chicken
Broiled New Potatoes
Honey Glazed Carrots and Green Beans

Wedding Dinner #4

Tomato and Cucumber Salad in Sour Cream
and/or
Mushroom Soup
Roast Pork with Rosemary and Garlic
Creamed Potatoes with Chives and Horseradish
Sweet and Sour Cabbage with Balsamic Vinegar

The Sweet Supper

Instead of a large, expensive wedding, many couples in Poland today prefer to wed quietly with a few select friends present, and then host a small reception called *cukrowa kolacja*, a sweet supper.

The sweet supper is part of a very old tradition among the nobility of Poland that dates back to the eighteenth and nineteenth centuries. It originated in the times when the bride and groom were officially "bedded down" by a select group of elders, who were chosen according to importance or closeness to the family circle. It was the job of these individuals to put the newly married couple to bed, and act as witnesses to their spending the night together, thus making the marriage official. Over the years, the custom changed and became an intimate gathering of a few select people to enjoy good food and wine at the end of the wedding feast. Towards the end of a wedding reception the bride and groom would invite a few of their very best friends to their private chambers, where they hosted another small, more intimate party. The focus of the gathering was a beautifully decorated table, laden with delicious desserts such as walnut and chocolate tortes, ice cream and other temptations, that were served with champagne or a sweet wine. The table was set with the finest china and crystal, complemented by fine table linens and fresh flowers. This special party then changed its focus again, and simply became the reception for an evening candlelight wedding conducted at an elegant hotel or restaurant. For the right couple, who wish for a very small wedding with only closest friends and family, the "sweet supper" can be an intimate and elegant affair.

Sweet Supper

Walnut Torte
Deep Chocolate Layer Cake
Almond Pastry
Cream Puffs
Chocolate Eclairs
Lady Fingers
Poppyseed Macaroons
Black Forest Cherry Crepes
Apple Crepes
Fresh Peach Ice Cream
Sweet Liqueurs
Champagne

Wedding Reception Entertainment

Entertaining guests after the wedding dinner has been the norm for centuries. Royal weddings are by definition sumptuous affairs, with all the trappings of grandeur and majesty. In previous centuries, wealthy and powerful families celebrated their newly-formed unions with parties that included jousting tournaments, huge banquets, and festivities that lasted for as long as two weeks. In the 1500s, tournaments and jousts were organized. Jugglers performed feats and jesters told jokes and generated laughter. By 1640, tournaments were no longer the main attraction. For the wedding of Katarzyna (Katherine) Radziwłł to the Lithuanian Lord High Steward Jerzy (George) Karol Hlebowicz, a hunt was held during the day. During the evening hours the night sky was aglow with fireworks. For his second marriage to Maria de Gonzaga, King Władysław IV organized a major theatrical production, complete with an opera. Poets penned sonnets and musicians created new music to celebrate the occasion.

Even humbler folk made sure that their guests were properly entertained. Whether the reception was held at home or at a local public inn, plans were made to ensure a rollicking good time. The musicians were asked to allow the guests to make requests for certain songs. Guests could take the lead in singing to the music. Or the leader of the band sang the first part of a tune and asked the guests to sing the refrain along with him. Or, the orchestra or band began playing a dance tune at a slow pace and gradually increased the tempo until the dancers were left breathless at the end.

Music is such an important part of the wedding event that a great deal of emphasis is placed on selecting a band or disc jockey for the reception, as well as musicians for the ceremony. The music sets the tone for the wedding traditions and festivities. As soon as you know the time and place of your wedding reception, start looking for the entertainment. Keep in mind your musical tastes and preferences, as well as that of your guests. What is important is that you make a good match between the style of the entertainer and the style of the party you would like. Some couples wish for a more restrained atmosphere or simple background music for socializing. Others prefer an energetic dance party and nothing but an experienced polka band will do. Before you pick your musicians be sure to hear them yourself. Be sure you know what you want and ask for it directly. Ask if they know traditional Polish music, especially for the oczepiny, if you are planning on having the custom as part of your wedding day. Have sheets with words and music if you would like the guests to sing along.

Oczepiny: The Unveiling and Capping Ceremony

Of all the customs associated with a Polish wedding, there was none more significant for a young Polish bride than the moment when the *czepek*—the cap of the married woman—was placed upon her head. This custom, called *oczepiny* (the unveiling or capping), is one of the most important and the oldest of Polish wedding customs. It is one wedding custom that has stood the test of time. Performed by all the different socioeconomic classes of Poland, it was a custom that was at one time prevalent throughout most of Europe, but disappeared eventually without a trace. Only Poland continued to uphold this very ancient tradition, and it continues to be kept alive in thousands of Polish-American weddings every year. It is *the* custom that makes a Polish-American wedding very special.

The removing of the veil (unveiling) and the placing of the cap (capping) is a symbolic moment for the new bride. It becomes a rite-of-passage from young woman to married woman. With the removal of her veil or wreath, and the placement of a cap or bonnet, she enters the ranks of married women. Throughout Poland and all of Europe, wearing a cap was a declaration, a statement, of being married. Just as wearing a wreath of flowers by a young girl was a symbol of virginity and the single, unmarried state, so a cap distinguished a woman as married. For every day wear, married women wore simple caps made of plain white fabric. For special occasions, a woman wore a very elaborate one, made of finer fabric, richly decorated with embroidery. Very often this cap was the one she had received on her wedding day during the capping ceremony.

The Czepek: The Marriage Cap

The marriage cap was usually a gift to the bride from her godmother. This was the norm if the godmother was still alive. The godmother made it herself or commissioned someone to make the cap for her goddaughter. Sometimes, it was the mother of the bride who sewed the cap. In the absence of any female relatives, the bride made it for herself or paid someone to make it for her. It was also appropriate for the groom to pay to have it made for his future wife.

Each region of Poland had a different variation on the style of the cap. Some were very elaborate and made of a variety of fabrics such as gold lamé, velvet, damask, satin, brocade, lace, or a combination of these materials. Some of the caps were made of silk, and heavily embroidered with gold or silver thread. Some were round, like a pillbox hat, only made of tulle and embroidered. Some tied under the chin with a big bow. Others tied in the back with a big bow. Regardless of the style, a lot of time, effort and money was put into making a beautiful czepek.

Witnessing a marriage in a wealthy noble family in the eighteenth century, a historian recorded: "the bride, in a lovely rose-colored dress and curled hair, anxiously anticipated her marriage cap because her father wanted her to receive both the cap and the tiara he was giving her, at the

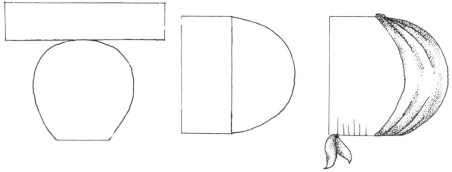

Pattern for bridal cap, the czepek.

same time. The cap was a gift from the groom, made by a top milliner in Warsaw called Lazarewicz. When the matrons gathered, the housemaid removed it from its box. It was made of costly lace and flowers and pink ribbon and underneath, according to current fashion, a diamond tiara. Her adoptive mother and a few respected ladies conducted the oczepiny with this lovely czepek and accepted her into the fold of married women."

Among the middle and poorer classes, the czepek varied in fabric and price but, of course, it was the best a family could afford.

In Śląsk, the cap was a piece of lace that fit the skull of the head and covered the forehead almost to the eyebrows. The lace was made at home on bobbins. Later on with the advent of machine-made lace and netting, the marriage cap was still worn in the same way but made from a piece of netting with small star motifs embroidered on the front that fitted across the forehead.

In the Kaszuby region, the cap was traditional in shape but very unusual and distinctive in fabric and embroidery. Two nunneries were responsible for making and embroidering the marriage caps. The nuns, who did delicate embroidery for the church, developed a very distinctive marriage cap that became popular throughout the entire region. The caps came to be called "złotogłow" - i.e., gold heads, because gold thread was used to satin stitch a design on black velvet or silk. The caps from this region were among the most expensive in the nation and available only to the very wealthy.

It is impossible to describe all of the variations of the cap within the scope of this book. However, many of the caps were based on the standard pattern that I have included in this chapter. This pattern can be enlarged and made into an authentic Polish czepek that matches the fabric of your bridal dress.

The marriage cap was generally made of two pieces of fabric. It consisted of a back piece which covered the back of the head and a front piece that framed the face. The bottom of the back piece was gathered. Sometimes this was done with the help of a ribbon, threaded through a small hem. The front piece could be very wide or very thin and made of a similar or different fabric as the back piece, or made of lace.

The czepek can be made from a variety of fabrics. Illusion is a fine, delicate nylon or silk mesh that is very soft and can give the czepek a soft and wispy look. This would be especially lovely if the bride chose a dress with an illusion neckline. It is available in white or ivory. Tulle is a fine mesh made from nylon yarns that are a little thicker than illusion. It is also less expensive than illusion. Point d'espirit, available in nylon and cotton, is a net with rectangular or circular dots woven at regular intervals. This small amount of pattern may be enough to eliminate the need for any embroidery. Another option is French net, a very strong, yet soft and sheer, net. The border of the czepek can be a simple lace. This can be a galoon lace, flounce lace, or simple edging, and can be used to finish the front or back of the bonnet. Many laces range from narrow trims to wide yardage. They are available in several forms and widths with the same or coordinating motifs. A trip to the fabric store will give you a good idea of the wide selection of fabric available.

A few years back a very good friend of mine was getting married and planned on having the traditional oczepiny. I offered to make her cap as a wedding present, an idea that she jumped on immediately. We went together to a large fabric and notions store, where we explored the specialty trims section. Her dress included beaded and sequined appliqués on the bodice and sleeves. She picked out a trim that was not exactly like her dress, but matched it in fabric and style. I bought a strip of the beaded material for the front border. For the back I bought a piece of white satin. The cap turned out lovely and added a special feeling to the oczepiny ceremony.

The Unveiling and Capping

The capping ceremony begins late into the night after the musicians have played a few sets of music and everyone has had an opportunity to dance and enjoy themselves. The bride makes sure that she dances with all her unmarried female friends before the capping ceremony. The master of ceremonies, or in today's time, the best man, decides when it is time to begin the unveiling and the capping. The band or orchestra gives a drum roll and the best man makes the announcement. The lights in the room are dimmed except for those on the dance floor.

In the olden days, the bride sat on a dough bin which had been turned upside down and covered with a sheepskin coat. The thick, woolly part of the sheepskin, considered a sign of fertility, was always placed outward. In today's time, a bench or chair in the middle of the dance floor facing the guests, will serve adequately. The maid of honor, usually designated to do the honors, stood behind the bride. The maid of honor was sometimes helped by the bride's new mother-in-law.

All the single girls stood next to and behind the bride and maid of honor to lend their support to this auspicious moment. The married women lit small candles and surrounded the bride and her single friends while her veil was removed and joined in the singing. As the orchestra or band began to play, the maid of honor began to remove the pins that held the veil or wreath in place.

There were many different songs that signaled the beginning of the ceremony. In the Łódź section of Poland the oczepiny always began with *Maryś, ach Maryś (Mary, oh Mary)* or the hop song, *Oj, Chmielu, Chmielu.* Very popular here in the United States was the Twelve Angels Song, sometimes known as *Rosnie Trawka* (The Grass Grows), or *Dwanaście Listeczek* (Twelve Leaflets). *Spadła z Wisni* was another popular song for the Oczepiny.

As everyone sings, the maid of honor, slowly and with great solemnity, removes the pins. As soon as the wreath or veil was removed from her head, the bride was completely surrounded by the unmarried girls who sang:

"Good evening, newest bride
Your wreath has fallen
Your bridesmaids are leaving you
But thank you for your friendship.
We wish you (name)
A happy life
May you be good to your husband
Love him truly
And in misfortune
Continue to help him."

While it was the role of the single girls to remove the veil or wreath, the task of putting on the czepek was relegated to a married woman. In olden days, the placing of the cap on the bride was a momentous event from which there was no turning back. The bride would even try to put off the event as long as possible. The first time the cap was placed on her head she threw it off, saying the cap didn't fit. One of the married women would take off her own cap, saying "Maybe this one will fit better," but the bride would refuse that cap also. The third time the cap was tried on, the bride had to leave it on her head as a sign of her acceptance into the circle of married women. At this moment and this moment only, she was officially a married lady. With the candles still in their hands, the womenfolk officially presented her to the wedding guests as a married lady by singing:

Everyone take a good look.
She was in a wreath and comes in a cap.

There was a sequence for dancing immediately after the bride received her czepek. First, the bride danced with the married women. All the married women took turns dancing with the bride as a sign of her acceptance into their ranks. In the Poznań region, this was usually done with the women standing together in a circle holding hands while one of them took the bride into the center and danced with her. When all the married women had danced with the newly capped bride, she danced with the married men, then fathers and brothers. After everyone had taken their turn, the groom claimed his bride for a slow dance.

In most Polish-American weddings the groom is also given a new hat as a symbol of his newly married state. It is generally covered with baby bottles or baby dolls or vegetables that have a very definite phallic suggestions to remind him of his new responsibilities. In all my research through hundreds of Polish books, I have only come across one instance of documentation with regard to placing a wreath on the head of a male at the oczepiny ceremony. Polish ethnograper Jan Piotr Dekowski writes "very rarely seen in Central Poland was a wreath for the male. This was done for fun and laughs. The wreath was made from nettle, juniper or thistle. Sometimes it was made from straw." His comment suggests that this custom did occur in other parts of Poland but unfortunately I was unable to locate further information and details such as when it was done or by whom.

Here in America the placing of a wreath on the groom was replaced by a hat. You can decide to go traditional with a wreath or stay with the hat. What is important is that it continues to be fun. A Polish-American wedding wouldn't be the same without it.

The Money Dance

The money dance was a custom original to Poland. It was also called the czepek dance, a dance that that took place after the oczepiny ceremony in country weddings. Guests would pay money for the privilege of dancing with the bride. There are many variations on how the money was collected. In some areas of Poland a plate was placed next to the bride and whoever wished to dance with the bride put some money in the plate. Sometimes the money was tucked into the bride's apron and was called the apron dance. In other regions, someone captured the bride's shoe and the money was placed in the shoe. Wherever or however it was collected, this money was a wedding gift to the couple with which to begin their housekeeping. In its place we now give bridal gifts or money envelopes. However, that's not to say it couldn't or shouldn't be re-instituted as a family tradition. The money could be donated to a church group, food shelter or some other charitable organization.

When the groom paid for the privilege of a dance with his new wife, it signaled their exit from the festivities. The dancing and having a good time continued long after the bride and groom had departed. To help the guests keep up their energy, another round of food was offered. Pastries and fruit were set out on a table for those who felt the need for more fortification.

Ideas to Borrow from the Past:

- Make a traditional cap for your unveiling and capping ceremony. No one wears the cap of the married woman anymore but it can be saved and made over into a small cap or bonnet for the christening of your firstborn. Wouldn't that be a nice tradition to start in your family?

- For guests attending your wedding who are not Polish American, you may want to briefly write up a flyer describing the custom. It helps people to understand just what is going on and get into the spirit of the event. It may also be helpful to have the music and songs available.

- Hire a Polish folk dance group dressed in Polish costumes to put on a small performance for your guests. Wouldn't it be fun if the group then stayed for a while and danced with the guests?

The Wedding Cake

The wedding cake has been part of wedding ceremonies from time immemorial. Today's wedding cake is believed to be derived from the Romans. A simple wheat cake or biscuit was baked and broken, and the first morsels were eaten by the bride and groom. The remainder of the cake was broken over the bride's head and the guests gathered up the crumbs and ate them. The cake, made of finely ground wheat flour, was a symbol of fertility and the earth's abundance. It supposedly guaranteed the bride and groom a life of prosperity and many children. This custom was carried on for centuries throughout Europe, including England and

Scotland. Over time the wedding cake underwent numerous changes. One of these culinary changes was icing the wedding bread, an influence brought on by the French. Eventually wedding cakes became the concern of a professional confectioner rather than the bride's mother or important female family members and friends. The cake became an object of fashionable show, complete with tiers, flowers and monograms.

The first documented record of a special bread served at Polish weddings dates back to the beginning of the thirteenth century. This was a sweet bread made from fine wheat flour and yeast. It was called a *kołacz* or *korowaj*. The name kołacz stems from the Polish word for "circle," and defines the traditional shape for the Polish wedding cake or bread. In ancient times it was a symbol that had special, magical powers.

The baking of the wedding bread was terribly important with special rules and regulations. The dough was very carefully prepared by the godmother of the bride or selected women who brought the finest flour and eggs and even a cherished bowl for mixing the ingredients. Half of the prepared dough was made into the wedding cake or bread itself, and the other half was used to adorn the top of the cake. Small clumps of dough were fashioned into birds, roosters, chickens or other farmyard animals. Sometimes hearts and flowers were made or figures of people (the bride and the groom) were placed on top. The older Polish wedding breads also had branches on them that were made of bread dough. In later years the top of the wedding bread was decorated with herbs and plants such as a wreath made of rosemary, green periwinkle and sweet smelling flowers. Roses were very popular. For winter weddings, evergreen herbs and plants adorned the cake. It was also decorated with birds, apples and nuts.

By the middle of the nineteenth century, even Poland was influenced to the popular wedding customs that were coming out of France and England. Writing about a wedding in 1830, Łukasz Gołębiowski indicated: "the cake for the wedding was in colors with cupids shooting into a heart, doves with roses and forget-me-nots in their beaks, or topped with the initials or monograms of the couple within a wreath of myrtle." The wedding bread was made as large or as small as desired. The wealthier population was able to afford breads or cakes containing an almond filling in the center. Another ethnographer noted that he saw an entire wedding cake made of marzipan. Marzipan is a confection of ground almonds, sugar and egg whites. Almond paste and fillings continue to be favorites in baked goods in Poland today.

Like the wedding cake of today, the wedding bread held center stage at the reception for all to see and admire. In some parts of Poland, especially

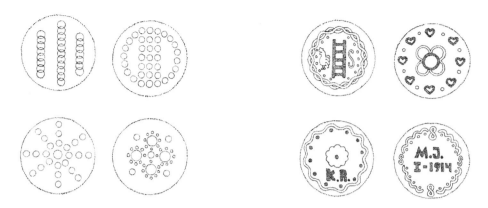

Decorations for top of wedding cake, Lowicz region, were simple at end of 19th century.

Motifs on wedding cakes were more decorative in Lowicz region in the early 20th century.

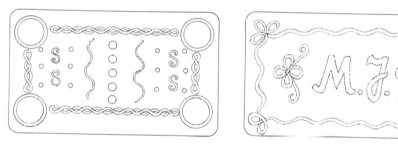

At left: *Wedding cake top from turn of century;* at right: *more elaborate decorations of early 20th century. Both from Lowicz region.*

the Białystok region, the bread was wrapped in a specially embroidered cloth that had been made just for that purpose.

As is the custom today, the cake was cut and served at the end of the wedding festivities. In old Polish tradition, the best man cut the wedding cake into smaller pieces. Before the cake was cut, however, six to nine lit candles were placed around the cake. The best man then made a small speech, extinguished the candles, and began cutting the cake. The first pieces of the cake were given to the bridal pair. Sometimes it was done differently. The bride cut herself a small piece of cake and then passed the knife to the groom. After cutting a piece for himself, the groom passed the knife to his best man, etc. In some parts of Poland the first pieces of bread cut after the ones for the bride and groom were sent to the parents of the bride and groom, then the bridal attendants, then to the rest of the guests and on down to the children. It was absolutely imperative for every

127

single wedding guest, even the smallest child present, to receive a piece of the wedding bread. The wedding bread was a symbol of their future bread together as well as that of their guests. The young couple had to share their bread with everyone as a sign of abundance and goodwill. The bread of life had to be delicious and it had to be abundant, and there had to be enough of it for everyone or it was considered a bad omen. If it ran out before everyone present had a least a bite, it augured poorly for the married life of the couple.

The bride has been capped, the cake eaten and the groom has claimed the last dance with his bride. It is time for them to leave their guests and depart for their wedding trip or take up residence in their new home. In Western traditions, it is time for the bride to throw her bouquet and wish the rest of the single girls the best of luck in meeting the man of their dreams. In recent years, the brides of Poland have been following this custom. However, older traditions dictate that the bride threw, not her bouquet (because she did not carry one), but her veil to the bridesmaids. Whoever caught it, would be the next to marry.

Chapter VI

Last Notes

Polish Marriage and Wedding Superstitions

- Rain on a wedding day means a successful and fruitful marriage.

- During the church ceremony, if a candle goes out on the groom's side of the altar, the groom will die first. If on the bride's side, she will die first.

- If the candles on the altar fail to burn brightly, sorrow will reign in the marriage.

- During the wedding reception, two candles are lit—one in front of the groom and one in front of the bride. The candle that stays lit the longest predicts who will live the longest.

- A grown woman should never sit on the edge of a table; her future husband will have a limp.

- If a girl finds a four-leaf clover and places it between her breasts, she will meet a man on the road who will become her husband.

- Thursday is a bad day to marry.

- To cry on one's wedding day is a good sign. If the bride doesn't, she will cry throughout her married life.

- A young maiden should never wear a carnelian ring or she will never marry.

- If a young maiden wants to get married she should secretly put the cap of a married woman on her head on New Year's Eve and dance around the room for a few moments.

- If a boy and girl are sitting next to each other and a spider falls between them, they will marry.

- A young maiden who sings at the dinner table will marry a stupid man; a bachelor who does the same will marry likewise.

- One should never give one's fiancé a lock of one's hair because the marriage will never take place.

- One's wedding clothes should never be dyed to another color or married life will be difficult.

- Scissors placed on the bed by either of the couple foretells argument in the marriage.

- Do not keep ivy (*Hedera helix*) in the house or there will be disagreements in the marriage.

- If a girl wants to know how long before she marries, she should go out to the forest in the spring and listen for the call of the cuckoo bird. She should call out loud, "Hey little cuckoo bird, how many years before my wedding day?" then she listens to the number of cuckoos. It will be that many years to her wedding day.

A Polish Welcome

Unfortunately there is no known painting or icon that depicts the full pageantry of the arrival of French princess Louisa Maria de Gonzaga to marry Polish King Władysław IV in March of 1646. It was, however, documented in the writings of an anonymous author in a text called *Ingress Tryumphalny do Warszawy*, which gives us an extraordinary picture of her arrival to the capital.

The unknown author writes that a magnificent two-tiered arch was erected over the city's main thoroughfare, Krakowskie Przedmiescie, not far from the Cracow Gate which was the entrance to the city. There were two tiers on both sides of the arch that held musicians who "kept up a joyful noise."

On hand to greet the new queen with drums, banners, and dressed in their finest clothes, was the entire city of Warsaw. Representatives of various guilds were dressed in their identifying livery "particularly the merchant's guild who dressed alike in a single color—yellow jackets with blue trim, sashed at the waist in yellow, feathers in their hats and all of them with muskets at their side." There was the king's honor guard, with banners of the dragoons and hussars. All moved to meet the new bride and future queen at the field, a quarter of a mile from the city gates. On the orders of the king, all the banners of the foot guard were left on the field in two rows. Eighty tents were erected on this field.

At eleven o'clock in the morning, in a carriage lined in red velvet, Duke Karl Ferdinand (brother of the king) arrived in the company of four dignitaries. At the same time, the retinue of Louisa Maria began to move towards the meeting place. Carried in a red velvet sedan chair, she was preceded by her senior lady-in-waiting, Reneé de Guébraint, who sat in a black sedan chair. Flanking both sides of Louisa's sedan chair were Krzysztof Opalinski, the Wojewod of Poznań (Governor of the Poznan Province), and the Bishop of Warmia, Wacław Lesczyński, on horseback. They had accompanied the future queen of Poland all the way from Paris.

At the moment that the queen's retinue met with that of Karl Ferdinand, a salvo was fired three times with muskets. After a brief greeting between the queen and her lady-in-waiting, they left their sedan chairs and entered the duke's carriage. The canopy of the carriage consisted of a heavily embroidered silver brocade fabric, trimmed on the edges with silver fringe and held up at the four corners with four silver eagles mounted on poles. The carriage was pulled by eight dapple-gray horses.

The people of Warsaw lined the road that led into the city and called out greetings to the queen. At the arch at the entrance to the city, the mayor gave a brief speech entrusting the city to the care of the queen.

The entourage continued forward. First to lead the parade and enter into the capital were the heralds in red *zupan* (long overcoat) and green velvet jackets. They were followed by the queen's foot guard and then by the most important magnates, nobles and minor princelings of the country, "everyone dressed in silver and gold, riding fabulous horses, harnessed richly in silver and gold, and followed by footmen carrying banners emblazoned with their family crests."

They were followed by the bishop from France and the bishop of Płock, who historically sat at the right hand of Polish kings. Immediately preceding the queen's carriage was her marshal with his staff in his hand. Surrounding the queen's carriage were twelve footmen in red velvet with gold trim and forty of the castle guards in yellow satin jackets with gold trim. Following the queen were sixteen trumpeters and behind them, held high, were the banners of France.

According to the anonymous author, the entire cavalcade moved towards St. John's Collegiate Church where the festivities ended. The next day the couple spoke their wedding vows and Louisa Maria de Gonzaga was crowned Queen of Poland.

Warsaw Wedding in 1725

This is a description of the wedding of one P. Łukasz with Katarzyna Millerówna on July 5, 1725 as written in the Warsaw Courier:

The weather predicted a fortunate life for the young couple. At 7 P.M. the wedding party walked to church accompanied by a march played by the musicians. The groomsmen were dressed in *żupans* with flowers pinned to their lapels. Surrounded by the groomsmen was the groom. There were more than ten bridesmaids, dressed so beautifully as to be a balm to the eyes. They did not look like town girls—more than one princess would envy the jewelry and baubles they wore on their foreheads, around their necks and on their ears. The bride's dress was white as snow. She did not wear any shiny jewelry: pearls mean tears and expensive stones can foretell misfortune. Her eyes, however, shined like stars. Aunts and cousins were dressed in jackets and even though it was hot and caused discomfort, they wore fox furs around their necks. The Franciscan priest said the Mass at the Church of Blessed Mary. The bride cried, which was seen as good, for it is better to cry at the wedding than complain your entire life. It is a bad thing for a bride to laugh at the altar.

Returning with great pomp from the church ceremony, the parents greeted them with bread and salt. Inside the bread were 100 shiny new *dukats*. The mother asked if the candles on the altar burned brightly. She broke down and cried with happiness when everyone assured her that they did, indeed, burn brightly. There were tables set up in four rooms and everyone was seated according to age. Everyone enjoyed the wonderful marzipan made by Chrystyana whose store is on Piwna street near the bake house.

After the meal, the men took to drinking and the women to dancing. Just as it was getting light, they capped Kasia and everyone offered their gifts: household items, wine cups, garments and a barrel of wine. The music played until everyone left.

The Diary of Marianna Malinowska Jasiecki

The following is an excerpt from the diary of Marianna Malinowska Jasiecki regarding the preparations and marriage of her oldest daughter, Rose.

Polwica, December, 1900

I've been so busy I've hardly had time to write in my diary these days. Rosie's wedding draws near and the house is constantly filled with young people and I still have many things to prepare. In September after the harvest festival but before Michael's (the writer's husband) name day celebration, I had the house freshened with new wallpaper and paint. Luckily, Grandma (her mother) has returned from taking the cure at Warbrunn and is helping me. We have lots of work. Rosie's trousseau is completed but the bridesmaid's dresses still have to be sewn as do dresses for Grandma and myself, as well as the wedding dress for the bride — loads of things to prepare.

Stasia (her sister-in-law)has gifted me with material for a dress, fabric which is not available to us here in the Poznań region. It is a beautiful French velour in a deep red cherry color which would be lovely against my dark hair. Stasia contends that the bride's mother must look equally lovely on the wedding day, especially if there are younger daughters in the home. An old and shabby looking mother would scare off any would-be suitors, in that they will think her daughters will eventually look old and shabby. So I will have a wonderful dress for Rosie's wedding. Grandma also received material from Stasia. Hers is a beautiful light gray cashmere.

Sophie, Maryna and Hedwig will be bridesmaids for their oldest sister. Their dresses will be similar in three different shades of blue. The fourth bridesmaid will be Haline Malinowska who is already eleven years old. Unfortunately, Helen Thomas has to be removed from the group making up the wedding party. (Helen broke the rules of good behavior when she spent the night alone with a man—making her socially unacceptable.)

The bride's wedding dress will, of course, be white with a long veil to the floor. I glue to my diary a separate list of the wedding trousseau of my daughter, Rose, beginning with the cost and then itemizing the table cutlery, china, linens for the table, bedding and personal linen.

I have truly tired myself out counting and writing out these items but this will serve me in the future when I will be preparing the trousseaus of my younger daughters. One must not lament the work involved. I will compile a list of Rose's entire wardrobe just before the wedding, when everything will be ready. After the wedding I will list the more important wedding presents. We will invite many guests for the wedding so there will be no lack of wedding gifts. Rosie's dowry is to be in the form of cash, which Michael will pay at the time of the signing of the marriage and it will be secured by notary to Boguliński (the groom) in Środa.

Rosie's fiancé is refurbishing the rooms that are to be theirs after the wedding. The lovely home has been in the Boguliński family for over two hundred years and its location is close to the city delights. Rose promises herself a very active social life which Thaddeus equally enjoys.

The young couple seem suited to each other. Both are tall and well formed, look good together, dance well and have similar sunny dispositions. Rose is very much in love with Thaddeus and enters the marriage wholeheartedly of her own free will. No one is forcing her to marry. They should be happy—God willing. I have stopped worrying about the bad luck that was prophesied about Rose by Mrs. Bogulińska on her deathbed. Perhaps it is just a silly superstition and not worthy of poisoning my thoughts. How happy Anulka would be if she were only in my shoes preparing a daughter for her wedding day!

Polwica, December, 1900

Advent has begun. Rosie's nuptials draw closer. I have so many demanding problems and preparations that it doesn't bear telling. Literally, I feel dazed. From morning to night I'm running from one thing to the next and when I lay down to sleep I'm still noting that I failed to do this or that or, much worse, that I forgot to do something. Most important is that the wedding dress is completed and the wedding invitations sent out. Now I have to attend to the overseeing of the kitchen for Christmas and all the family holidays until the New Year.

There will be approximately seventy guests for the wedding, most of whom will be coming only for the wedding and reception. Thaddeus's side of the family will stay at the Boguliński estate. My side of the family will stay at our home. Anthony and his children will come for the entire holiday. The Thomas's from Żabikowa and the Ziemniewicz's from Wolsztyn will also arrive for the wedding. Sophie Werczynska will be staying with us for a few days. Michael's family from the Wągrowiecki district have also promised to come—two sisters and one brother, who unfortunately, we do not get to see very often. Rose has also asked a few of her friends from her boarding school and they will be staying with us for a few days.

The wedding will take place at our parish church in Śnieciska at four in the afternoon. It will be celebrated by our dear pastor, Reverend Dr. Ludwik Marzewski. An excellent orchestra from Środa has already been hired. The wedding reception will, no doubt, last till dawn.

In regards to future trousseaus that I will be preparing for my younger daughters, I must accurately write down what Rose receives from us in the matter of personal clothes. In keeping with the custom of young ladies, the bride will distribute her dresses among her younger sisters. The lesser valued items will be given to the servants and parlor maids and the most threadbare and unneeded items will be relegated to the poor. She will leave her family home with a new wardrobe suitable for a young married woman. Many of these items have already been assembled. Grandma has become critical of these clothes claiming that I am needlessly spoiling her with these modern clothes. Rose is vain and loves to dress. This is an undeniable fact and even worries me a little. But I certainly can't allow the possibility of my daughter having to buy herself new dresses or coats within the next few years. Her bride clothes must last for a few years (unless, the young wife decides to buy herself something extremely modern on a whim or through sheer fancy). Her personal clothes should last ten years and the bed and table linens should last into the next generation and if the family fails to increase and the house doesn't grow any larger, then her entire trousseau should certainly last her a lifetime. These are the rules and I comply with these rules as I prepare my daughter's trousseau. Kitchen items should also be part of the trousseau but this is understood and I will not be listing those. Michael is also of the opinion that one cannot skimp on a trousseau and doesn't even grimace when I present him with a new bill. Who do we work for if not for our children? For their trousseaus we will not skimp and attempt to give them all we can, being equally generous from the oldest Rose to our youngest Hedwig.

Rose also receives a complete set of furniture for her parlor: a couch, six arm chairs, an oval table, lamp and an expensive painting. The furniture is made of walnut covered with a gold flowered damask,

135

the material coming from Egypt, as well as a suitable rug. This suite of furniture is really very beautiful.

Rosie's wedding dress is beyond beautiful. It was sewn in Aniela Remblow's dress shop in Poznań. It is of the latest fashion made from a luxurious white India silk covered with tiny pleats which elegantly enhance Rose's slender figure. The bodice is also pleated with a round slightly low neckline(a deep neckline would be unsuitable for a wedding). Below the tightly fitting bodice, the waistline is of French Valenciennes lace and overlaps a little on the skirt which has a flounce of illusion all along the bottom. The sleeves are long and of pleated lace all the way to the elbow and covered at the shoulders with large epaulettes made of illusion. From the back, two large sashes from pleated material fall to the hem line and are attached to the back with large rosettes. The skirt does not have a long train. The veil, made of illusion, is three yards long and pinned to her forehead with a wreath of myrtle and orange blossoms. Rose looks stunning in her wedding dress. With the dress is a white cloak trimmed in white fox fur because of the time of the year. The weather between Christmas and the New Year tends to be extremely cold and calls for warmer clothes. Shoes for the wedding will be white with high heels and narrow toes, as is the current fashion.

The dresses for the bridesmaids will be sewn alike, only each in a different shade of blue. The skirts will have flounces. My dress of dark cherry velour was also sewn by Remblowa. The sleeves are puffy. The neckline is cut low and embroidered with flowers around the décolletage. For the trip to the church, I ordered a hat to match the outfit. The crown of the hat has flowers to match those on the bodice. The hat is something beautiful but cost a fortune! Neither Michael nor Grandma can guess what I paid for it and I don't even dare disclose the amount to my diary. In the end, the material for the dress cost me nothing, only the sewing, so that I didn't have to scrimp on the hat. I take comfort in the good advice given me by my sister-in-law—that in looking good myself, I also improve the future of my daughters. A lovely appearance by the mother foretells what her daughters will look like in the future—an important issue for would-be suitors.

For her granddaughter's wedding Grandma will look appropriately noble. The light gray India cashmere from Stasia is sewing up beautifully as it is a thin wool-like silk. Our dresses will harmonize beautifully: the white dress of the bride, the blue dresses of the bridesmaids, the pearl of my mother, mine of cherry and, of course,

Michael's frock coat. For Steffie and Jani (youngest daughters) I had rose colored dresses with flounces made up. We should all look good together. Summertime would have called for a different look with brighter colors of yellow and crimson. In those colors Rose had some summer blouses and dressing gowns made up. Against her dark hair and beautiful complexion, it looks good. On me these garish gypsy colors hardly look elegant.

I am unable to write adequately about clothes but I suspect that in the future, my children, it will be pleasant for you to see with your own eyes, the dresses from these years. For the wedding we will have the photographer from Środa take a picture of the bridal pair and all the gathered guests. It will be a valuable memory for both Rose and ourselves.

Polwica, January 1901

With the departure of my brother and the entire family and after bringing the house back to its normal functioning, I can quietly sit down at my desk in order to write the details of the wedding of our oldest daughter, Rose, who on December 29, 1900 became the wife of Thaddeus Boguliński from Środa.

Our eldest daughter has left her family home to begin establishing her own family within the family home of her husband. This was a difficult moment for us to live through. It is good that Rose will not be living too far away from us and that we will be able to see her frequently.

It feels empty without Rose. I don't know how I will survive when Stasia will leave for grammar school in April. It's a terrible thing—to be separated from your children. And that, unfortunately, the future will bring and for that there is no choice.

Our Rosie's wedding day fell on a day that was not too cold but fairly cloudy. It didn't snow. The road to Śniecisk was very good because this year there is very little snow, so much so that Michael is worried already for the crops. For the wedding it was opportune because we rode splendidly in horse-drawn carriages. The entire wedding retinue consisted of twenty-six carriages.

We had a house full of guests for Christmas but we all managed to fit. This wasn't the first time that I have discovered that Grandma has a natural born talent for organization: she arranged everyone so that everyone was satisfied and didn't complain of any discomfort. As Lady Bejmowa says, "In a little cup, the oatmeal tastes better."

The crowd in the family gathering room failed to cause anyone concern. There were few small children because our youngest is already a year old and is always so agreeable. Anthony's boys and our Steffie are already a little older and not so troublesome. So it was crowded but merry and it seems as if the time passed pleasantly for everyone. For the wedding there were close to seventy people and seventy-six people sat down to the tables besides the servants, coachmen, etc. who all ate in the servants' hall.

First I'll write about the wedding day. For the cooking I hired a renowned cook recommended to me from Dolska, a Mrs. Kozłowa, celebrated for her elegant cuisine. She has been organizing affairs for the better families for quite a few years and does not concede to any cook from Poznań and has this virtue—that she will not get drunk—which happens to practically every cook. Mrs. Kosłowa arrived a week before the wedding, leaving only for Christmas day and returning immediately afterward and prepared everything with the help of our cook and hired girls. So that on the day of the wedding, as guests began to arrive, we offered bouillon, beef tenderloin and steak roll-ups. Before leaving for the church everyone could help themselves to coffee and donuts (we made over four hundred), cookies, babas and fruit such as apples, pears, oranges, bananas, walnuts and candied fruits. After the coffee we left for the church and immediately on our return we had the wedding supper.

We had turtle soup with small meat pastries in the French style, salmon in mayonnaise, pike in aspic, a dish with turkey and lobster sauce, baked venison and various vegetables and compotes followed by pineapple ices, a layered cake and lastly, black coffee and liqueurs. With the meal there was an excellent Hungarian wine, madeira, tokay and champagne with dessert. During the dancing there was a continuous supply of coffee, wine, cooling drinks, candy, cakes and tortes. The wine flowed in a stream, the overall mood splendid. At 2 a.m. a second supper of hot bouillon and two meat courses was served and after that the traditional "sweet supper" - that is, the wedding cake along with other tortes and sweet baked goods with accompanying drinks and champagne.

In the morning as guests were leaving, everyone was offered coffee, tea, homemade drinks, various baked goods and meat pastries. Mrs. Kozłowa shared her recipe for turtle soup(I ordered and received the

turtles at Leitgeber in Poznań) and am writing it down to remember:
for six people, one pound of turtle meat and a pound and a half of beef.
Boil the meats in an appropriate amount of water with soup herbs,
spices and salt. To the stock is added a browned roux and a half of a
glass of Madeira wine or Tokay. Cut the turtle and beef meat into fine
chunks and add to the soup tureen. One can also add finely chopped
green parsley. This soup is truly delicious.

Following tradition, Rosie was dressed for her wedding day by
single, unmarried women—her younger sisters, her friends from
boarding school, the two young Ossowidski girls from Śrem and
another young lady—the daughter of Josie Ziemniczow (the older ones
are already married). The parlor maids also helped. Haline
Malinowska as an eleven-year-old was too young to participate.
Thaddeus doesn't have a sister, so from that side of the family there
was no one to help dress the bride. Helen Thomas, pretending to have
a headache, remained in her room, which was one way to get out of the
situation and didn't even go to church, but willingly helped set and
decorate the tables which, I must admit, turned out beautifully.

After the bride was dressed, the groom personally handed his
bride's wedding bouquet to the bridesmaids, as well as those of the
bridesmaids. The bouquets were superb: roses, carnations, orchids,
lily-of-the-valley, and lilacs all surrounded by ferns and the delicate
greenery of asparagus. The bride's bouquet was entirely white. The
bridesmaids had rose colored bouquets surrounded by a pleating of
organdy. In the wedding procession the bridesmaids were accompanied
by the groomsmen: the groom's two brothers, Simon and Marcel;
Thaddeus's friends Ksawery Matecki and Vincent Ziemniewicz, Josie's
son, to pair off with Haline Malinowski.

In the parlor I arranged to have two pillows from the couch placed
on the floor so that the young couple would have a place to kneel while
receiving the parental blessings. For this very moving and solemn
occasion all the guests gathered in the parlor. For the blessing,
Michael and I stood next to one another. Next to me stood Mr. Vincent
Boguliński. Because Mrs. Boguliński is no longer living, Mrs. Natalia
Ostrowska, Thaddeus's aunt, sister to his deceased mother, a congenial
woman of the gentry from the Leszczynski district, took her place.

Rosie descended the stairs surrounded by her bridesmaids.
Thaddeus met her and together they approached us, passing through
the aisle formed by two rows of assembled guests. How beautiful our
daughter looked in her bridal white! My eyes filled with tears when I

looked at Rose as a young bride. Both fathers were no less moved but just like men, kept their countenance. Throughout the parlor the ladies dabbed their eyes with their hankies. The young pair kneeled before us to accept the parental blessings. I gave Rose a small bundle wrapped in white cloth: a tiny piece of bread, a pinch of salt and a gold coin. She should have these as she marries so that she may never lack for these items in her lifetime. Mrs. Ostrowska, substituting for Thaddeus's deceased mother, hung a necklace with a gold locket on Rose's neck that had previously belonged to Izabella Boguliński. We offered our parental blessings—mutual love, long life and God's protection on the formation of a new family on this day.

After the blessings everyone left for the church. There were carriages, chaises, coaches as well as sleighs, even though we had little snow. There were also a lot of servants and tenant farmers traveling on foot. Michael released everyone from work for the day, like on Sunday, and ordered a repast be prepared for our workers. The larchwood church in Śniecisk was festively lit and decorated. The entire altar was covered with sweet smelling white hyacinths grown by our gardener just for this day. The marriage was celebrated by the Reverend Dr. Ludwig Marszewski with the assistance of his two vicars. From the choir loft Veni Creator was sung solo, and a violin and organ played.

Rosie was escorted to the altar by her father—proud and moved—handing her over to her husband before the altar. Thaddeus was escorted to the altar by his aunt, Natalia Ostrowska. The young couple approached the altar. Rose spoke her marriage vows loudly, without hesitation and didn't cry at all, as is frequently the custom. Oh, how I remember that I wasn't this brave at all at my own wedding—but the younger generation is different. The four pairs of bridesmaids and groomsmen looked becoming—the bridesmaids dresses sewn alike but in various shades of blue truly looked lovely. The smallest bridesmaid, Haline, stood next to the bride in the palest blue, and Sophie, the last and the tallest, in the darkest blue. Haline's groomsman was my nephew and Haline's cousin, Vincent Ziemniewicz. Hedwig was paired with Marcel Boguliński, Marina with Ksawery Matecki and Sophie with Simon Boguliński.

After the church service Michael and I hurried home so that we could greet the bridal couple at the door with the traditional bread and salt. The newly married couple returned last at the end of the entire wedding cavalcade. The coachmen, standing on the carriages, cracked their whips. After offering the bread and salt, the house servants came forward to offer their good wishes to the bridal pair—the guests had already offered their wishes as they exited from the church. Then we all sat down to a splendid wedding supper which I have already described.

During the meal there were many toasts offered—as is customary during these occasions. The first toast offered to the newly married couple was offered by our good friend, the celebrant of the marriage, Father Ludwig Marszewski, a truly gifted religious. He spoke of the wedding at Galilee and the greatest power on earth—love. Then Mr. Vincent Boguliński offered wishes of good health to Michael and myself and to Rose, thanking us for the honor of kinship with our family and giving him our Rose as his daughter-in-law and as mistress of their home. Dearest Mr. Carl Rzepecki gave a rhyming toast to which my brother Anthony also answered in verse. Father Marzewski took the floor again and with great enthusiasm offered good health to out dear Grandma, mothers and grandmothers, the models of Polish matriarchy. He tied this talk to the young bride and her grandmother, wishing the granddaughter the attainment of her Grandmother's virtues and the love of her entire family. This speech touched everyone. It was a moving picture when our mother was surrounded by all her children and grandchildren, thanking her for everything that she has done for her family throughout her lifetime. Everyone then stood and we all sang together a traditional wedding toast.

After the wedding feast, the dancing began which, except for a break for supper, continued playing till dawn. Towards morning Rosie went to the young ladies parlor, removed her wedding attire, dressed in a new tailor-made suit and her new beaver fur and privately said good bye to us so as not to disrupt the festivities (she was at this moment the most emotional) and with her happy and laughing young husband left in Boguliński's carriage for the railway station to begin her honeymoon journey to Vienna. The couple should return from the trip soon.

In the meantime we said goodbye to all the wedding guests and family who had gathered for the wedding (my friend Sophie Werczynska stayed the longest. I am greatly worried about her for the poor thing is ill and went to a lot of trouble to travel here to Polwica). Finally, with the help of Mr. Vincent we transported all of Rosie's trousseau to Środa and our gardener took over some beautiful flowers to decorate the apartment for their arrival. Their rooms were freshened earlier and are tastefully and elegantly arranged. Our Rose will walk into her own apartments with a young and agreeable husband. Our prayers, Grandma's and mine, go with her: Be happy, dear Rose, in your married life for the longest time! Fulfill all your marital obligations honestly and willingly! May the dear Lord bless you, my dearest and oldest daughter!

And now for memory's sake I will write down the wedding presents that Rose received, most importantly from the family. There was jewelry: a brooch with pearls, a ring with a large sapphire, a pearl pin in the shape of a swan, a Swiss watch with a long gold chain. In silver serving pieces: two silver sugar bowls, a pitcher for coffee, a pitcher for tea (both matching an oval silver tray), another large silver tray, an oval silver-plated vase, two silver plates for cakes, two dishes for fruit, two large silver vases, a decorated rectangular silver plate, a pair of silver candelabra each with twelve candles, two small modern silver-plated candlesticks, a pair of silver candelabra each with eight candles, two round silver napkin rings, two oil paintings in gilded frames (one a winter landscape, the other a still life with fruit), an inlaid ebony chest, a mirror in a silver frame for her dressing table. Thaddeus received a gold cigarette case from his father and brothers, engraved with the date of his marriage. From his uncle he received an English rifle for hunting. From Michael he received a good horse for horseback riding, so that they have a pair, for Rose took her favorite mare, Alma.

The wedding went off beautifully. The guests left Polwica fully satisfied. May it be a good omen for her future life!

Appendix 1

Traditional Polish Baby Names

Every nation possesses it's own treasury of names from which to draw on when a new child is born. The history of names used in Poland can be divided into two major periods. The first group are native names categorized as Old Polish or Slavic in origin. These were used from the most ancient of times until the acceptance of Christianity. During this early period, people lived in nomadic clans and tribes, hunting and gathering, and faced numerous environmental dangers as well as tribal enemies. The selection of a name for a newborn infant during this time was a truly serious affair and a highly emotional moment. It would have to be a strong name, a name with honor, rich with history and promise, for in those days it was believed that a child would develop the characteristics of whomever or whatever he/she was named after. These distinctive, ancient names are not easily translatable into English.

The second group of names stems from the time Poland accepted Christianity in 966 AD until the present. The Church required individuals to receive baptismal names which had a Christian significance. At their baptism, when they were "born again," early Christians assumed new personal names—invariably the names of exemplary people and saints who had gone before them. These are names that are found in the Old and New Testaments. The church has appointed certain days on the calendar as belonging to certain saints. Thereafter, throughout the Middle Ages in Europe, an infant was customarily named after the saint upon whose feast day he or she had been born. This was at one time a widely observed rule in Poland.

If the name was suitable and pleased the parents and family, it was used. If the parents wanted another name, the name of a saint whose feast day had already passed was chosen. This was done so that the infant could come immediately under that saint's protection. Those who did not adhere to the rules chose a name the family desired without any regard to the calendar, but the name was always a Catholic one derived from the Old or New Testament or from the lives of the saints.

The custom of naming a child for the name of a saint led to the celebration of that day as the child's name day or feast day. In many parts of Europe such as Spain, Italy, France and Poland, the custom of celebrating the "name day" was more critical than celebrating the day of birth. The name day, called *imieniny* in Polish, was the celebration of the feast of the saint who's name was received in baptism. The Poles considered this "baptismal saint" a special patron throughout life. The saint after whom he or she was named became, in essence, the child's hero or heroine. As a child grew older, he or she was made familiar with the stories and legends of his or her own special saint. Children were instructed to pray to the saint every day for help and guidance throughout their lives, and to be inspired by their loving and kind acts towards others. Subsequently, mothers and fathers took great care in naming their children.

This chapter is intended to help you become acquainted with Polish first names. Picking the name of a child is as important today as it was centuries ago, and should be given much thought and consideration. It is a child's name that will set him or her apart from others. It is often the first word that a child will speak. Many third and fourth generation Polish Americans who are identifying with their origins are changing both their first and last names back to the original family names. As they are having their own children, they are choosing names that fit with their ethnic heritage, either as first or middle names. Ask about the names of grandparents and great-grandparents. One of the key needs of young people today is a source of identity, of knowing who they are and where they came from. They need heroes and heroines in their lives, whether it's their grandmother who traveled alone in steerage to begin a new life in America, or a person who lived in the fourteenth century and died in service to the sick and poor.

Christian name diminutives are used within the family and by close friends as terms of endearment. Sometimes they become the pet or "nickname" used by friends. Some of the ancient Polish spellings are quite interesting and would make for unusual and unique names.

There are thousands of saints, many with the same first name. Many feast days vary from diocese to diocese or from one religious order to another. The feast date(s) given is that most commonly accepted and is usually the date of the saint's death or the date of the translation of his/her relics.

A very useful calendar with all saints' names is the *Polish Heritage Art Calendar*. Information on where to find this calendar is listed in the Source chapter.

Girl's Names

Agata. Agatha. Greek. "Good."
Seen in Polish writings in the 13th century as *Agata* and *Jagata*, this was a favorite name in the small country villages of Poland until the 18th century. It came into favor again in the 1970s. St. Agatha was venerated in Italy and Germany as the patron of fire lightning and bread. She was put to death for refusing to put aside her religious beliefs. In Poland there are many traditions associated with the feast of St. Agatha, such as the blessing of salt, bread and water.
Diminutive: Agatka
Feast Day: February 5

Agnieszka. Agnes. Greek. "Pure, chaste." Patroness of children and
   young girls.
St. Agnes was a young Roman girl who was martyred at the age of 13 in the 4th century for refusing to deny God and marry a pagan.
Popular in Poland since the time of the Middle Ages, this name has seen many variations in spelling including *Agneta*, and *Jagnieszka*. It was given to many Polish princesses from the Piast line as well as girl children born in small country villages.
Diminutive: Agunia, Jagunia, Agusia
Feast Day: January 21

Anastazja. Anastasia. Greek. "Who will rise again."
St. Anastasia was a noble woman who used her wealth to aid Christians being persecuted in Rome. Known in Poland since the time of the Middle Ages, this name been spelled *Nastazyja* in the past.
Diminutive: Nastka, Nastusia
Feast Day: December 24

Aleksandra. Alexandra. Greek. Feminine form of Alexander. "Helper of Men."

There are many saints with the name of Alexander. It was used in Poland since the 14th century and continues to enjoy popularity.

Diminutive: Alka, Ala, Ola

Feast Day(s): February 26, March 18, August 28

Aniela. Angela. Greek. Feminine form of Greek *Angelos* and Latin *Angelus*. "Messenger, Angel."

This is a name that became popular in the 18th century primarily through the Ursuline nuns. The founder of the order was Angela Merici, who gathered twenty-eight women together and named the group the Ursulines in honor of St. Ursula.

Diminutive: Anielka

Feast Day: January 16

Anna. Ann. Biblical/Hebrew. Derived from Hannah which means "Grace." Patroness of childless women.

According to the Christian tradition, St. Anne was the mother of Mary, mother of Jesus Christ. It has always been one of the most popular girl names in Poland. According to a study done in Cracow in 1989, it was the second most popular name, second only to Katarzyna (Catherine).

Diminutive: Ania, Hania, Anka, Hanka

Feast Day: July 26

Apolonia. Appolonia. Greek. Feminine form of Apollo meaning "Belonging to God." Patroness of dentists.

In more recent times this name has been shortened to *Pola* and was popular for country girls. World renowned Polish-born actress Pola Negri was named Apolonia Chałupiec at birth.

Diminutive: Apolonka, Polonka

Feast Day: February 7

Barbara. Barbara. Greek. "Stranger, foreign." Patroness of miners, architects, artillerymen and sailors.

St. Barbara died at the hands of her own father for refusing to deny her faith. In Poland she is invoked against lightning and an untimely death. Her feast day is celebrated by the miners of Poland with a special mass and celebration. A favorite name beginning in the 14th century, it was the name of numerous queens of Poland.

Diminutive: Basia, Barbarka
Feast Day: December 4

Bożena. No English translation. Slavic. "Blessed by God."
This is a very prevalent name in Poland. It is thought to be Czech in origin and is sometimes spelled with two n's.
Diminutive: Bożenka
Feast Day: March 13

Brygida. Bridget. Celtic. "Strong, strength."
This name shows up in Polish records as *Bryda* in 1265 and as *Brygitta* in 1465. It became well-liked because of St. Bridget of Sweden who founded the Bridgettine Sisters.
Diminutive: Brygidka
Feast Day: July 23

Cecylia. Cecilia. Latin. Feminine form of Cecil. "Blind, dimly sighted one." Patroness of church music and church musicians."
Written as *Cecylija* in 1265. Became more prominent in the 18th century.
Diminutive: Cylka, Cyla
Feast Day: November 22

Danuta. Donna. Lithuanian. Derived from the Latin Donata. "God-given."
Diminutive: Danka, Danusia
Feast Day: June 24

Dorota. Dorothy. Greek. Feminine of Theodore. "God's Gift." Patroness of brides, florists and gardeners.
In the Middle Ages, Dorothy was a prevalent name in Germany and among the Czechs. Its popularity slowly transferred to Poland, becoming especially popular in Cracow and remains so today.
Diminutive: Dora, Dorotka
Feast Day: February 6

Edyta. Edith. Old English. "Happiness."
St. Edith was a young English girl who took religious vows and spent her lifetime caring for the sick and poor, especially lepers. A name that is currently enjoying a revival in Poland.
Diminutive: Edytka

Feast Day: September 16

Elenora. Eleanor. Origin is thought to be Greek. Derived from Helen. "Light."
Many great English queens were named Eleanor and its many variations. It was also used by a Polish queen, Elenora Maria, wife of King Michael Wiśniowiecki of Poland.
Diminutive: Elenorka
Feast Day(s): February 21, August 18

Elżbieta. Elizabeth. Biblical/Hebrew. "Oath of God." Patroness of pregnant women.
According to the Bible, Elizabeth was the wife of Zachary and mother of St. John the Baptist. It is a prominent name throughout the centuries, appearing in Polish documents as *Elisabet* (1222) and *Elesbeth* (1307).
Diminutive: Ela, Elka, Elunia
Feast Day: November 5

Emilia. Emily. Latin. Feminine form of Emil. "Excelling."
This was a name also favored by Polish queens and princesses. Maria Emilia was the daughter of Ziemowit, a Mazowian king who ruled that part of Poland. It was popularized through Polish literature in the 18th and 19th centuries.
Diminutive: Emilcia, Emilka, Mila
Feast Day(s): April 19, May 3, June 30

Ewa. Eve. Biblical/Hebrew. "Giving life."
Wife of Adam, mother of all people, Eve was supposedly created from the rib of Adam.
Diminutive: Ewka, Ewina
Feast Day: December 24

Felicja. Felice, Felicia. Latin. Feminine form of Felix. "Happy, lucky"
A well-known name in Poland in the 18th century but no longer so. *Felicissima* (the most happy) was another version of this name in Poland.
Diminutive: Fela, Felcia, Felka
Feast Day(s): January 24, April 27

Franciszka. Frances. Teutonic. Feminine form of Francis. "Free."
A well-liked name in 18th century Poland. It became even more popular in the United States when Frances Xavier Cabrini became the first citizen

of the United States to be canonized as a saint. She established the first American convent and orphanage among Italian immigrants. Known as the patron saint of emigrants and migrants.
Diminutive: Frania
Feast Day: November 13

Genowefa. Genevieve, Jennifer. Origin either Celtic or Germanic "Race of women." Patroness of Paris.
A name that gained in popularity in Poland since its first appearance in the 15th century.
Diminutive: Genia, Gieńka
Feast Day: January 3

Gertruda. Gertrude. Old German. "Spear, strength."
Came to Poland in the Middle Ages. It was popular in the regions bordering Germany.
Diminutive: Gerta
Feast Day: November 16

Grażyna. No English translation. Lithuanian. "Beautiful."
Made popular by poet Adam Mickiewicz in his 1823 poem "Grażyna." It was especially popular before and after World War II.
Diminutive: none
Feast Days: April 1, July 26

Halina. Helene. Greek. Derived from Helen. "Bright one."
Many heroines in 19th century Polish literature helped to bring this name to prominence.
Diminutive: Hala, Halka, Halinka.
Feast Day: July 1

Helena. Helen. Greek from Helene. "Bright one, shining one"
In Greek mythology, Helen was the daughter of Zeus and the most beautiful of women. She is the Helen of Troy in Homer's *Iliad*. It appears in Poland under a variety of guises including *Alena* (1386) and *Elena* (1265). It was most popular in the 19th century and given to Helena Modrzejewska (1840-1909), Polish-born actress of international fame.
Diminutive: Helcia, Hela
Feast Day: August 18

Irena. Irene. Greek. "Peace." Patroness of Peace.
Did not appear in the Polish language until the 18th century and then caught on very quickly.
    Diminutive: Ira, Ircia, Irka
    Feast Day: April 3

Iwona. Yvonne. Old German. Feminine version of Iwo. "Yew wood or archer."
A newer name in Poland, sometimes shortened to Iwa, pronounced Eva.
    Diminutive: Ivonka
    Feast Day(s): April 24, May 19, May 23

Izabela. Isabella, Isabel. Spanish/Portugese. Supposedly derived from Elizabeth. "Pledged to God."
The true origin of this name is not completely clear. It is thought to come from the Spanish Isabel or the biblical Jezabel. It has been the name of many queens of Spain and its popularity spread throughout all of Europe, including Poland. The first recorded Izabel in Polish records was in 1519 when King Zygmunt I and his wife Queen Bona Sforza baptized their first child Izabella. The name reached more prominence in the 17th and 18th centuries.
    Diminutive: Iza, Izia, Bela
    Feast day: March 16

Izydora. Isidora. Greek. Feminine version of Isidore. "Gift of Isis."
A name taken up from the Greeks by the Romans and then by Christians. Caught on in the 18th and 19th centuries.
    Diminutive: none
    Feast Day: April 4

Jadwiga. Hedwig, Heddy. Old German. "Safety in battle."
Another name that traveled to Poland from Germany probably with Hedwig of Meran (1174-1243) wife of King Henryk the Bearded. After the king's death, she entered the convent at Trebnitz. She was canonized in 1243 and became the patroness of Silesia. Hedwig was also the name of the Queen of Poland (1374-1399), daughter of Louis of Hungary.
    Diminutive: Jadzia, Jaga, Iga
    Feast Day: October 16

Janina. Jane. Latin. Feminine version of John. "The Lord has mercy."
The name is given in honor of the many saints named John. A newer name in Poland that became more prevalent in the 1850s.
Diminutive: Janka, Janeczka
Feast Day: June 24, December 27

Joanna. Joanne or Joanna. Latin. Feminine version of John.
St. Joan of Arc is the heroine of France. As a young girl she helped the King of France re-conquer his country. She was burned at the stake for heresy by her enemies. Joanna can be counted among Poland's favorite girl names. It appears in Polish chronicles in many interesting forms including *Johanna* (1265) and *Jenna* (1275) and the more simple *Jena* (1372). Its newest version appears as Janina.
Diminutive: Joasia, Jasia, Asia
Feast Day: May 30

Jolanta. Yolande. Greek. "Violet flower."
Early documentation spells this name as *Jolenta* (1277). Jolanta was also the name of a Polish princess who was beatified in 1827. It gained prominence in the later years chiefly through the central character of Jola in "The Maids from Wilno" by Iwaskiewicz.
Diminutive: Jola, Jolka
Feast Day: June 15

Józefa. Josephine. Hebrew. Feminine version of Joseph. "Increases."
The name is given in honor of St. Joseph, foster father of Jesus Christ and husband of Mary. It was popularized by Josephine de Beauharnais (1763-1814), first wife of Napoleon. The name spread throughout Europe and was especially well-liked in small country villages.
Diminutive: Józia, Józka
Feast Day: March 19

Julia. Julie, Julia. Latin. Feminine version of Julius. "Downy, soft beard."
There were many saints by this name. St. Julia who lived in Carthage in North Africa was murdered for refusing to honor false gods. The name was brought to prominence in the Western world through William Shakespeare's "Romeo and Juliet." The play was first seen in Poland in 1799 and became a favorite name up until World War II.
Nickname: Julka, Julcia, Jula

Feast Day(s): May 22, June 19, October 1

Justyna. Justina. Latin. Feminine version of Justine. "Just."
This name dates back to the 14th century in Poland but was used more frequently in the 19th century and carried into the 20th.
Diminutive: Justynka
Feast Day(s): April 14, September 26

Katarzyna. Catherine, Katherine. Greek. "Pure."
One of the most popular names for girls in Poland. St. Catherine of Labouré, a French nun who gave the world the Miraculous Medal. On her feast day, unmarried girls would drop hot, melted wax on water, study the figures created by the hardening wax and make marriage predictions. If the wax hardened into something resembling an ax or a tree, their future husband would be a forester, etc. It was a name that was also popularized by Catherine of Sienna, a Dominican visionary.
Diminutive: Kasia, Kasieńka
Feast Day: November 25

Karolina. Caroline. Old German/Teutonic. Feminine version of Carl/Charles. "Strong."
Popular in 19th century Poland and currently enjoying a revival.
Diminutive: Karolinka, Karolcia, Karolka
Feast Day: November 4

Kinga. No English translation. Hungarian form of the Old German name of Kunegunda.
This name came to Poland with Kinga (1224-1292), daughter of Belli IV, King of Hungary, when she married Polish King Boleslaus the Shy. She was also a patron of the Poor Clares who had an abbey in Stary S1cz in Southern Poland.
Diminutive: Kinia
Feast Day: July 24

Klara. Clara, Clare, Claire. Latin. "Bright, shining, clear."
This very old-fashioned name was very widespread in Poland. St. Clare was the 13th century founder of the order of Poor Clares, a Franciscan order of nuns who serve the poor and needy.
Diminutive: Klarusia, Klarcia
Feast Day: August 11

Kornelia. Cornelia. Latin. Feminine version of Cornelius. "Like a horn."
Used infrequently in Poland in earlier years but slowly gaining strength.
Diminutive: none
Feast Days: February 2, March 31, September 16

Krystyna. Christine. Greek. Feminine form of Christ. "Anointed."
St. Christine was a martyr who was thrown into water with a mill stone around her neck, yet did not drown. The name appears in the 14th century in the unusual form of *Kierstyna*. It became more prominent as a result of Polish literature, especially the writing of Henryk Sienkiewicz.
Diminutive: Krysia
Feast Day: July 24

Leokadia. Lydia, Lilian. Greek. "Light, bright,clear." Feminine form of Leocadius.
A prevalent name in the 19th century and currently gaining more prominence.
Diminutive: Loda, Lodzia, Leosia
Feast Day: December 9

Liliana. Lilian, Lillian. Latin. Derived from lily, a flower.
From the most ancient of times, the lily has been a symbol of purity and among the most favorite of flower names. The name is given in honor of the Blessed Virgin, whose symbol is the white lily. In the 14th century, the old Polish spelling was *Lilija*.
Diminutive: Lila, Lilka
Feast Day(s): September 4, December 8

Lucyna. Lucia, Lucy. Latin. "Light." Feminine form of Lucian.
Used more frequently in the 19th century. St. Lucy was the daughter of wealthy parents who gave away all her possessions to feed the poor.
Diminutive: Luca, Lucka, Lucynka
Feast Day: December 13

Ludwika. Louisa. Old German. Feminine form of Louis. "Renowned fighter."
St. Louise de Marillac (1591-1660) eatablished the Sisters (Daughters) of Charity, a religious order dedicated to caring for the poor and providing them with hospital care. A much loved name long ago.
Diminutive: Ludka, Lusia

Feast Day: March 15

Magdalena. Magdalen. Hebrew. "From Magdala."
In the New Testament, Mary Magdalen appears as one of Jesus's most devoted followers. She attended His burial and went to anoint His body only to find the tomb empty.
Nickname: Magda, Madzia
Feast Day: July 22

Małgorzata. Margaret, Marjorie, Margot. Greek. "Pearl."
This name appears in 12th and 13th century Poland as *Margareta*, *Margarita*, or *Margata* as well as other variations. It was the 7th most popular name in Poland in the 17th century. It declined in popularity in the 18th century, completely fell out of mode in the 19th, and regained its popularity in the 1960s and 1970s. There were also a variety of shortened names that appeared also such as *Greta* (1352).
Diminutive: Gosia, Małgośka
Feast Day: July 20

Maria. Mary. Hebrew. "Rebellious."
As the name given to the mother of Jesus Christ, it was initially thought to be too sacred to use but gradually became one of the most popular female names in the Christian world. In the 1700s, during the war with the Swedes, the Polish people attributed the successful defense of the shrine at Częstochowa to Mary. There are many feasts honoring the Blessed Virgin under various titles and any one of these can be chosen as a personal feast day. In Poland the most popular occurs on the Feast of the Assumption of the Blessed Virgin Mary.
Diminutive: Maja, Marynia, Marysia
Feast Day: August 15

Marta. Martha. Aramaic. "Lady, Mistress of the House."
According to the Bible, Martha was the sister of Mary and Lazarus, whom Jesus raised from the dead. She is known as the patroness of housewives which stems from her solicitude towards Jesus when He visited the family home. It was a favorite name during the period between the two world wars.
Diminutive: Marcia, Martunia
Feast Day: July 29

Melania. Melanie. Greek. "Black, dark skinned."
Encountered more among Polish Americans than in Poland.
Diminutive: Mela, Melcia
Feast Day: December 31

Monika. Monica. Uncertain origin but thought to be Greek. "Counselor."
St. Monica was the mother of St. Augustine, a brilliant individual who defended the Christian faith. His mother helped him overcome a life of debauchery and self indulgence. It was a name that was used in the 15th century but gained more prominence after World War II and then in the 1960s and 1970s.
Diminutive: Nika
Feast Day: August 27

Natalia. Natalie. Latin. "Birthday of the Lord."
Found in Polish records in 14th and 15th centuries.
Diminutive: Natalka, Talka, Tala
Feast Day(s): July 27, August 26, December 1

Pelagia. Pelagia. Greek. "From the sea." Feminine form of Pelagios.
A name seen more frequently in the 19th century than it is today.
Diminutive: Pela, Pelunia
Feast Day: October 8

Regina. Regina, Queenie, Reyna. Latin. "Queen."
This is a name given in honor of the Blessed Virgin Mary, Queen of Heaven (*Regina Coeli*). A well-liked name in small villages in southern Poland.
Diminutive: None
Feast Day: August 22

Renata. Renee. Latin. Derived from Renatus. "Reborn."
Cecylia Renata of France was the first wife of King Władysław IV and popularized this name.
Nickname: Rena, Renatka, Renia
Feast Day: November 12

Róza. Rose. Latin. A flower.
Popularized by St. Rose of Lima, patroness of Peru. A name that goes back in antiquity but does not appear in Polish archives until 1470.

Diminutive: Rózia
Feast Day: August 23

Sabina. Sabina. Latin. "Member of the Sabine Tribe."
The Sabines were a tribe in central Italy. In an effort to provide wives for the citizens of Rome, mass kidnapping of the Sabine women was arranged. In literature it came to be known as the the "Rape of the Sabine Women." St. Sabina was a wealthy Italian woman who was converted to Christianity by her slave, St. Seraphia. Both women were put to death for their faith in the first century. It is a name that is being given in Poland more frequently today than in previous centuries.
Diminutive: Saba
Feast Day: August 9

Salomea. Salomea. Hebrew from the word *shalom*. "Peace."
Salomea was one of the women who ministered to Jesus. It appears in Polish records as *Salome* (1146) and *Salomeja* (1252). Many queens and princesses of Poland had this name and was frequently given to infant girls up until the 19th century.
Diminutive: Sala, Salka, Salcia.
Feast Day: November 19

Stephania. Stephanie. Greek. Feminine version of Stephen. "Crowned."
St. Stephen was the first martyr of the church. He was stoned to death outside the walls of Jerusalem. In his memory, the people of Poland threw oats and wheat at their parish priest on his feast day. As a girl's name, Stephanie did not catch on in Poland until the 19th century when the name appeared in popular literature.
Diminutive: Stefa, Stefcia, Stefka
Feast Day: December 26

Teodora. Theodora. Greek. "God's Gift." Feminine version of Theodore.
Known in the 15th century and again in the 18th century and then fell out of favor.
Diminutive: Teodosia, Dosia
Feast Day(s): April 1, September 11

Teresa. Theresa. Origin not completely clear but believed to derive
from the Greek. "Harvest, reaper"
Due to the popularity of St. Teresa of Avila and St.Thérèse of Lisieux,
Theresa has been very popular among Catholic families including those
in Poland.
Diminutive: Terenia, Tereska, Renia
Feast Day(s): October 1, 15

Wanda. Wanda. Slavic/Old German. "The wanderer."
Some sources feel that this is probably a Slavic tribal name of the
Vandals, a Germanic tribe. It is found in some of Poland's earliest
chronicles and became more widespread in the 17th and 18th centuries.
Diminutive: Wandzia
Feast Day: June 23

Weronika. Veronica. Latin. "True image."
According to legend, a young woman named Veronica wiped the face
of Jesus on his way to the Crucifixion and was left an imprint of His
features on the cloth. The Polish pronunciation sounds very much like the
French Veronique.
Diminutive: Weronika
Feast Day(s): January 13, February 4

Wiktoria. Victoria. Latin. Feminine version of Victor. "Conqueror."
While Polish records indicate the existence of the name in Polish records
in the 13th and 15th centuries, the name really never took off until the
Victorian Era when everyone was naming their daughters after England's
Queen Victoria (1837-1901).
Diminutive: Wika
Feast Day: December 23

Zofia. Sophia. Greek. "Wisdom."
The French form of Sophia is Sophie. At one time one of the most
popular names in Poland.
Diminutive: Zosia, Zoska
Feast Day: May 15

Boy's Names

Adam. Adam. Biblical/Hebrew. "Mortal, man of the earth." Patron of gardeners.

From the Book of Genesis, Adam was the first man on earth created by God. It is a name known in ancient Polish documents since the 12th century. It was the name of one of Poland's greatest poets, Adam Mickiewicz (1798-1855), and Adam Stefan Sapieha (1867-1951), bishop of Cracow.

Diminutive: Adaś, Adasiek

Feast day: December 24

Aleksander. Alexander. Greek. "Defender and Helper of Men."

A very popular Polish name over the centuries, it was spelled as *Aleksandr* or *Aleksender* in the 15th century.

Diminutive: Alek, Olek

Feast day(s): March 18, August 28, December 1

Aleksy. Alexis. Greek. "Defender and Helper of Men." Patron of wanderers and beggars.

St. Alexis was a Roman who lived as a hermit who devoted his life to good works. There were many miracles wrought in his name. Often seen as a shortening of Alexander. Known in Poland in the 14th century.

Diminutive: Alek

Feast Day: July 17

Andrzej. Andrew. Biblical/Greek. "Manly." Patron of fisherman and spinsters.

Andrew was one of the twelve apostles, a fisherman, who followed John the Baptist. In Poland, there were two versions of Andrew, *Andrzej* and *Jędrzej*. Andrzej became the more popular version that stayed in the Polish language. On the eve of this feast day, young unmarried girls would try to make predictions about their future husbands through various techniques.

Diminutive: Andrzejek

Feast Day: November 30

Bartłomiej. Bartholomew. Biblical/Hebrew. "Farmers son." Patron of beekeepers, butchers, tanners and cheese merchants.

Bartholomew was a disciple of Christ, one of the original twelve apostles. It was a very popular name in the 16th centruy in the Tatra mountain region of Poland. It is a name that frequently shows up in Polish folk songs and Christmas songs.
Diminutive: Bartek, Bartosz
Feast day: August 24

Bolesław. (No English translation). Slavic. Roughly translated it means "He who can attain great glory."

This was a name tied to the Piast dynasty that generated many kings of Poland. It was a name that was lost for many years and then returned to popularity in the 19th century with the resurgence of interest in Slavic names.
Diminutive: Bolek
Feast Day: August 19

Bogdan. No English translation. Slavic. Roughly translated it means "Gift of God."

This is also a very ancient Polish name with roots in the early formative years of the Polish state. There were a variety of spellings for this name but two forms remained over the centuries: *Bogdan* and *Bohdan*.
Diminutive: Bogdanek
Feast day(s): March 19, July 17, August 31, October 2

Bronisław. Bronislaus. Slavic. Derived from two clauses meaning "to protect" and "glory/fame."

This is a name that has its origins in very early Poland and was at one time a very popular name for boys. It is less frequently given today in favor of more modern names.
Diminutive: Bronek
Feast Day: September 1

Chrystian. Christian. Latin. "Belonging to Christ."

This name was also spelled *Krystyjan* in the 13th century and tended to be given in the north of Poland which experienced a Germanic influence.
Diminutive: None
Feast Day: June 12

Cyryl. Cyril. Greek. "Lordly."
This was a very popular name in the Balkans throughout the centuries and gradually spread to Poland.
Diminutive: None
Feast Day(s): March 18, June 27

Dominik. Dominic. Latin. "Belonging to the Lord."
St. Dominic (1170-1221) was the founder of the Dominican religious order. Dominicans established their monasteries in Poland in the 13th century. This is a name that has been renewed in Poland after a long absence.
Diminutive: Domek, Domeczek
Feast Day: August 8

Edmund. Edmund. Old English. "Happy Protector."
There were many Englishmen who became saints of the church as priests and theologians. It was a name that spread to Poland and became popular in the 19th century and the period between the two world wars.
Diminutive: Mundek, Mundzio
Feast Day(s): October 25, November 16, November 20

Feliks. Felix. Latin. "Happy."
This was the name of many popes throughout the history of Christianity. It was very popular in the 16th and 17th centuries.
Diminutive: Felek
Feast Day(s): July 21, July 27, November 20

Filip. Philip. Greek. "A Lover of Horses."
As the name of one of the twelve apostles, this was a popular name throughout the Christian world. It appears in Polish archives in the 15th century as Filip and Pilip.
Diminutive: Fil, Filek
Feast Day: May 3

Florian. Florine. Latin. "Flowering." Patron of brewers, chimney sweeps and soap boilers. Protector of those in danger of fire and flood.
The cult of St. Florian the martyr widened in Poland at the end of the 12th century when his relics were brought to Poland and laid to rest at the Wawel Cathedral in Cracow. Statues of this saint can be seen throughout Poland near rivers, lakes, and bridges.

Diminutive: None
Feast Day: May 4

Franciszek. Francis. Teutonic/Old German. "Free." Patron of animals.
This is a name made popular by St. Francis of Assisi (1181-1226) who gave the world the custom of the manger scene at Christmas time. He is one of the most popular saints in the Roman calendar. He lived a life of poverty and love caring for the sick and needy. Francis was a name that was extremely popular in the 19th century and can still be found among the older generation in small country villages.
Diminutive: Franek
Feast Day: October 4

Frederyk. Frederick. Teutonic/Old German. "Peaceful ruler."
Found in Polish chronicles at the beginning of the 12th century, Frederyk became especially popular in western Poland where it bordered Germany.
Diminutive: Fredyk
Feast Day: July 18

Grzegorz. Gregory. Greek. "Vigilant watchman." Patron of singers and students.
The Feast of St. Gregory was traditionally celebrated in Poland on the day of his death, March 12th. It was practically a holiday for elementary grade pupils in Poland. It was a prominent name over the centuries and even more so after World War II.
Diminutive: Grzesiek
Feast Day: March 12

Gustaw. Gustav. French form of the Swedish name *Göstaf*. "Staff of the gods."
Derived from the name Agustus, the name did not appear in Poland until the 19th century mostly due to the influence of literature. It was the name for a character in a very popular work by the Polish poet Mickiewicz called "Dziady."
Diminutive: Gustek, Gucio
Feast Day: August 2

Henryk. Henry. Teutonic/Old German. "Ruler of the home."
St. Henry the Emperor founded monasteries and dioceses, encouraged missionary activity, and lived an exemplary life. It was, at one time, one

of the most favorite boy's names in Europe. It was the name of kings in England, France, Germany and Poland.
Diminutive: Henio
Feast Day: July 15

Ignacy. Ignatius. Latin. "Fiery one."
When the Jesuits brought the cult of St. Ignatius Loyola (1491-1556) to Poland and established their order, the name became very widespread.

Diminutive: Ignacek
Feast Day: July 31

Iwon. Ives. Teutonic/Old German. "Archer." Patron of lawyers.
St. Ives was a priest, pastor, lawyer and judge in his lifetime. He spent his life caring for the sick, feeding the hungry and ministering to the poor. The name is infrequently given in English speaking countries but enjoyed immense popularity in Poland and other Slavic countries.
Diminutive: None
Feast Day: May 19

Izydor. Isidore. Greek. "Gift of Isis."
Isidore of Spain worked all his life as a laborer but devoted his entire life to prayer. As a result he is called the patron saint of farmers and farm laborers. A well-liked name among the Greeks, Romans and Christians.
Diminutive: Izydorek, Dorek
Feast Day: May 10

Jacek. Hyacinth. Greek. A flower.
The first of the flowers with this name were said to have sprung from the blood of Hyacinthus, a Greek youth, accidentally killed by Apollo. St. Hyacinth (c.1200-1257) was one of the first saints of Poland. He was a Dominican who founded the first Dominican monastery in Poland. The name was a favorite in the 18th century.
Diminutive: Jacuś
Feast Day: August 17

Jakub. Jacob. Hebrew. "He who supplants."
In the Old Testament, Jacob is the brother of Esau. Jacob impersonates Esau at his blind father's deathbed by covering his hands with a goatskin. The English variant of Jacob is James. St. James the Apostle was a fisherman. He and his brother John were mending nets when Jesus called

to them "Come, follow me." It is a name that has remained steadfast as a popular name for boys over the centuries.

Diminutive: Kuba, Jakubek

Feast Day: July 25

Jan. John. Biblical/Hebrew. "The Lord Has Mercy."

John the Baptist began preaching in the wilderness of Judea and baptized his followers in the River Jordan. A universally popular given name for boys in Poland throughout the centuries. Between the 14th and 15th centuries every eighth man in Cracow carried the name of John. In 1978, Cardinal Karl Woytyla took the name John Paul II when chosen Pope of the Catholic Church.

Diminutive: Janek, Jasiek

Feast Day: June 24

Jerzy. George. Greek. "A farmer, one who tills the soil." Patron of England, knights, armorers and archers.

St. George, a knight and killer of dragons had a very large following in the Middle Ages. Besides being a much-loved name in Poland, it was equally favored in Russia, Lithuania, Czechoslovakia and Germany.

Diminutive: Jerzyk, Jurek

Feast Day: April 23

Józef. Joseph. Biblical/Hebrew. "Increases."

In the Bible, Joseph is the son of Jacob and Rachel. He is also the husband of the Blessed Virgin Mary and the foster father of Jesus. This name appears in various forms throughout the centuries in Poland without the diacritical mark above the letter "o" as in *Josyf* (1498), *Jozef* (1234) and *Jesyp* (1491). It was the most frequently given name in the 18th and 19th centuries. The cult of St. Joseph was popularized by the Bernadine monks and the Jesuits.

Nickname: Józefek, Józek

Feast Day: March 19

Juliusz. Julian. Latin. "Downy, Soft Beard."

Pope St. Julius I worked diligently to defend the faith against heretics in the 4th century. It was a well-liked boy's name in Poland. One of Poland's most famous romantic poets was Juliusz Słowacki. Another luminary carrying the name was Juliusz Kossak, an outstanding Polish painter.

Diminutive: Julek
Feast Day: April 12

Karol. Charles. Teutonic/Old German. "Strong." Patron of apple orchards and seminarians.
Charles is the English version of this very old German name which spread throughout Europe largely due to Charlemagne (742-814). The Polish version comes from the Latin version of Carolus.
Diminutive: Karolek, Lolek
Feast Day: November 4

Kazimierz. Casimir. Slavic. "Bringing peace." Patron of Poland and Lithuania.
Two major Polish figures contributed to the popularization of this name. The first was the Polish King Kazimierz the Great (1310-1370) who brought peace and prosperity to Poland after many years of strife, and St. Kazimierz, a Polish prince who devoted his brief life to prayer and love of the poor. When he died at the age of 26 in 1484, many miracles occurred at his tomb. He was canonized in 1521.
Diminutive: Kazik
Feast Day: March 4

Klemens. Clement. Latin. "Merciful."
Clement was the third pope after St. Peter to rule the Church and is honored as a martyr. It was a favorite boys name in Poland throughout the centuries and had a variety of spellings including *Klement* (1311) and *Kliment* (1411).
Diminutive: Klimko
Feast Day: November 23

Konrad. Conrad. Teutonic/Old German. "Courageous advice."
A very popular name in Germany during the Middle ages and was adopted by Poland. It was a name that could be found among kings of Mazowsze and Silesia.
Diminutive: None
Feast Day: February 19

Konstanty. Constantine. Latin. "Constant, steadfast."
St. Constantine was a Cornish prince who gave up his crown to become a monk. It was used in the 13th and 14th centuries in Poland, especially

164

in the eastern regions, probably due to the influence of Constantine the Great, the first Roman Emperor.
Diminutive: Kostek
Feast Day: March 11

Krystian. Christian. Greek. "Christlike."
Throughout the centuries there have been various spelling of this name in Poland including *Krystyjan* and *Chrystian*.
Nickname: Krystek, Krys
Feast Day: December 4

Krzysztof. Christopher. Greek. "One who carries Christ." Patron of bachelors, horsemen, travelers and police officers.
Among the most popular of boys names in Poland from World War I on.
Diminutive: Krzysiek
Feast Day: July 25

Leonard. Lennard, Leonard. Teutonic/German. "Strong as a lion." Patron of prisoners, the mentally ill and birthing mothers.
St. Leonard was a Frankish lord who spent the major portion of his life working among captives and prisoners. The cult of St. Leonard(6th century) was spread by the Cistercian monks. The name appears in Polish documents in the 12th century as *Leonard* (1193), and later as *Lenart* (1399) and *Lenhart* (1399). It was especially popular in Poland in the Podlesie and Mazowsze regions as well as in Lithuania.
Nickname: None
Feast Day: November 6

Leszek. Les. Slavic. "To act cunningly."
Polish etymologists are unsure of the precise origin of this name, knowing only that it shows up in Polish documents in various forms in the 12th and 13th centuries and may derive from the very ancient name of Lech.
Diminutive: Lesio
Feast Day: June 3

Longin. Longin. Latin. "Long."
The name derives from St. Longinus, a Roman legionnaire who was to have pierced the side of the Christ at the Crucifixion. He later converted

and died a marytr's death. His name was popularized in Poland by author Henryk Sienkiewicz, as one of the heroes in *With Fire and Sword*.
Diminutive: None
Feast Day: March 15

Lucjan. Lucian. Latin. "Light."
This is an unusual and rare form of the name Lucius. It was used infrequently in Poland until the 19th and 20th centuries.
Diminutive: Lucek
Feast Day(s): January 7, February 11, June 13

Ludwik. Loius, Lewis. Teutonic/Old German. "Renowned fighter."
Louis the Great of Hungary (1326-1382) was ruler of Poland from 1370 until his death. However, the name gained prominence with Louis the XIV, King of France.
Diminutive: Ludek
Feast Day: August 25

Łukasz. Lucas, Luke. Latin. "From Lucania." Patron of artists and doctors.
St. Luke, the Evangelist, the author of the third Gospel, was a Greek doctor. While this name appeared in old Polish archives, it has gained the most popularity within the last twenty-five years.
Diminutive: Łukaszek
Feast Day: October 18

Maciej. Matthias. Hebrew. "Gift of the Lord."
One of the most popular names in Poland from very ancient times. It was especially well-liked in the small mountain villages of Podhale in southern Poland. It's popularity is also reflected in some of the male characters in Poland's finest literature.
Diminutive: Maciek
Feast Day(s): January 30, February 24, May 14

Marcin. Martin. Latin. "Warlike." Patron of beggars, wine growers and innkeepers.
St. Martin of Tours was one of the most popular saints of France. There are many legends surrounding this individual including the one where upon meeting a naked man, he gave him his coat and soon afterwards had a vision in which Christ was wearing the coat. The name became prominent

in Poland after World War II but given throughout Poland's history to some of its finest scholars, authors and historians.
Diminutive: Marcinek
Feast Day: November 11

Marek. Mark. Latin. "Warlike." Patron of writers, notaries, basketmakers and glassmakers.
The name dates back to the time of ancient Rome with Marcus Aurelius and emperor Marcus Tulius Cicero. It became a Christian name through St. Mark, the author of the gospel according to Mark. His symbol was the lion.
Diminutive: Mareczek
Feast Day: April 25

Mateusz. Matthew. Biblical/Hebrew. "Gift of the Lord." Patron of tax collectors and customs officers.
The apostle Matthew wrote the first book of the New Testament. A cherished name in southern mountain regions of Poland known as Podhale.
Diminutive: Mateuszek
Feast Day: September 21

Maksymilian. Maximilian. Latin. "The Greatest."
Maximillian Kolbe was a Franciscan priest who offered his life in place of a younger man with a family at the Nazi concentration camp of Auschwitz. He died in 1941 and was canonized in 1982.
Diminutive: Maks, Maksymek
Feast Day: August 14

Michał. Michael. Biblical/Hebrew. "Who is like the Lord." Patron of policemen and warriors.
According to the bible, Michael the Archangel led the heavenly army against the forces of evil and became the patron of Christian warriors. In the Middle Ages, he was the patron saint of knights and his name became the leading one for boys. In those years the name was spelled *Michal* (1220), *Michial* (1394) and *Mechel* (1441). It was also popular in the Russian territories.
Nickname: Misiek
Feast Day: September 29

Mikołaj. Nicholas. Greek. "Victorious one." Patron saint of Russia.

In the 12th century the name appeared in Polish documents as *Nicolaus* and in the 13th and 14th centuries as *Nichol* and *Mikołojek*. St. Nicholas is one of the most popular saints in Christendom. The name became dear through the legendary Saint Nicholas, Bishop of Myra, patron saint of little children. Very popular in Poland during the Middle Ages and patron saint of young maidens, children, schoolboys, bakers and others. His feast day was considered a special holiday by sheperds and believed to be a day of protection against wild animals, especially the wolf.

Diminutive: Mikołajek
Feast Day: December 6

Paweł. Paul. Latin. "Little."

A widely used name in all Christian lands from the time of the Middle Ages until today. It was the name of seven different popes as well as Russian emperors. St. Paul wrote fourteen of the books of the New Testament and is honored with St. Peter as the cofounder of the Holy Roman Catholic Church.

Diminutive: Pawlik, Pawełek
Feast Day: June 29

Piotr. Peter. Greek. "Rock."

In the Bible, this was the name given to Simon, the man who made his living as a fisherman in the sea of Galilee. Jesus renamed Simon as Cephas, the Aramaic equivalent of the Greek word that means Peter (rock) in English. Jesus said : "On this rock I will build my church...and I will give you the keys of the kingdom." St. Peter was the first bishop of Rome.

Nickname: Piotrek
Feast Day: June 29

Rafał. Raphael. Hebrew. "God's Healer."

St. Raphael is one of the three archangels mentioned in the Bible. The name shows up in Polish archives in different forms including *Rafael* (1224), *Rachał* (1424) and *Refael* (1435).

Diminutive: Rafałek
Feast Day: September 29

Roch. No known translation. Unknown origin. Patron saint of contagious diseases.

A very old fashioned Polish name. According to legend Roch was an individual living in the 14th century who devoted himself to care of the sick, curing large numbers simply by making the sign of the cross over them.
Diminutive: None
Feast Day: August 17

Ryszard. Richard. Old German. "Strong Ruler."

Richard will always be a name that evokes images of Richard the Lion-hearted and Shakespearean plays. It takes on many forms in Poland over the centuries. These include *Rychard* (1222), *Rykard* (1212) and *Rejchart* (1385).
Diminutive: Ryś, Rysiek, Rysio
Feast Day(s): February 7, April 3, October 25

Roman. Roman. Latin. "One from Rome."

Originally Romanus, the name belonged to a Roman who lived as a hermit and developed a following. It was known in Poland in the 12th century as well as in Russia and the Byzantine Empire. Currently enjoying a renewal in Poland due to the renowned Polish filmaker Roman Polanski.
Nickname: Romek
Feast Day: February 28

Stanisław. Stanislaus. Slavic. Roughly translated means "stands for glory."

This is one of the most popular Polish names for boys since ancient times and has not diminished over the centuries. It is found in many forms in Polish documents such as *Stacher* (1442) and *Stanek* (1242). It's popularity was due to Polish saints: Stanisław Szczepanowski, bishop of Cracow c. 1030-1079 and St. Stanisław Kostka. The latter was a young man who vowed to become a Jesuit. When his family forbade the vocation, he walked three hundred and fifty miles to Rome. He received Holy Orders when he was 17 years old but died within a year.
Diminutive: Staszek, Stach, Stasio
Feast Day(s): April 11, August 15

Stefan. Stephen, Steven. Greek. "Crowned."

St. Stephen was the first martyr of the Church. Not only a popular name in Poland, but also in Hungary.

Diminutive: Stefanek, Stefek
Feast Day: December 26

Szczepan. Stephen. Same as above.

Szymon. Simon. Biblical/Hebrew. "Obedient"
St. Simon was one of the twelve apostles. A very common and well-liked name in Poland from the time of the Middle Ages until the 18th century and enjoying a revival at this time.
Diminutive: Szymek
Feast Day: October 28

Sylvester. Sylvester, Silvester. Latin. "From the wooded area."
New Year's Eve in Poland is called Sylwester after this saint who was Bishop of Rome in 314. He recognized Christianity and ended persecution against Christians.
Nickname: Sylwek
Feast Day: December 31

Tadeusz. Thaddeus, Thad. Biblical. "Courageous, wise." The name appears in shortened forms in old Polish records as Tadej (1339) and Tadaj (1430). It was more popular in Lithuania, once a part of Poland. St. Thaddeus was one of the lesser known of the twelve apostles.
Diminutive: Tadek, Tadzio
Feast Day: October 28

Teodor. Theodore. Greek. "God's gift."
St. Theodore was put to death for refusing to denounce his faith.
A very well liked name in Poland for many centuries.
Diminutive: Dorek
Feast Day: February 7

Tobiasz. Tobias. Biblical/Hebrew. "The Lord is good."
Used in Poland from the 13th through the 18th centuries but less so in modern times.
Diminutive: None
Feast Day: September 9

Tomasz. Thomas. Aramaic. "Twin."
The name of one of the apostles, known as "Doubting Thomas," who refused to recognize the risen Christ unless he could see and feel the marks of the Crucifixion. It was the name of some of the most famous religious men throughout the centuries such as St. Thomas Beckett, archbishop of Canterbury; St. Thomas Aquinas; St. Thomas More.
Diminutive: Tomek, Tomko
Feast Day(s): July 3, January 28, December 29, June 22

Walenty. Valentine. Latin "Valiant." Patron of engaged couples.
Once prominent name for Polish men which later fell from favor.
Diminutive: Walerek
Feast Day: February 14

Wawrzyniec. Lawrence. Latin. "Laurel."
St. Lawrence was a martyred deacon who developed a following in Europe. A favorite name for boys among the Polish nobility.
Diminutive: Wawrzek
Feast Day: August 10

Wincenty. Vincent. Latin. "Conquering one."
A name made famous by St. Vincent de Paul, a Frenchman who founded the Vincentian Congregation, a society of priests devoted to missionary work. It was also the name of one of Poland's most famous chroniclers, Wincenty Kadłubek, who was also bishop of Cracow. He was beatified in 1764.
Diminutive: Wicek
Feast Day: September 27

Zachariasz. Zacharias, Zachary. Hebrew. "Remembered by God."
St. Zachary was the father of St. John the Baptist. A name that was popular among the Orthodox Slavs.
Diminutive: None
Feast Day: November 5

Zygmunt. Sigmund. Old German. "Victory, triumph."
A very old Polish name often handed down through the centuries to princes in line for the Polish throne. It appears to have come to Poland through the Czechs. There were a variety of spellings through the centuries including *Zygmont* (1433) and *Sigismund* (1438).
Diminutive: Zyga, Zyguś
Feast Day: May 2

Pronunciation Guide

a as in father
1 as in the French word "bon"
e as in whey
i as the e in jeep
o as in oh
ó as the two o's in loop
u as in suit
y as the i in kid
c followed by any vowel except for i is pronounced ts
c followed by i or accented as ć is pronounced like the ch in church with the i sound stressed
ch is like the ch in loch as pronounced like a Scot
cz is pronounced like the ch in choo-choo
dz is pronounced like the J in John
dż like g as in hinge or j in jam
l as in ale
ł as like the wl in howl with a pronounced w sound
ś or s followed by an i is pronounced ssh
sz as in the sh of sheep
w as a v
z as in zebra.
There is no q, v or x in the Polish language.

Appendix 2

Music

Serdeczna Matko

Kto Się W Opieke

Pobłogosław, Jezu Drogi

Po - blo - go -slaw, Je - zu dro -gi, tym, co Se - rce Twe ko - cha -ja. Nie - chaj skarb -ten

cen -ny, dro - gi, na wiek wie -kow po - sia - da - ja.

Witaj Krolowo nieba

Wi - taj, Kro - lo - wo nie - ba i Ma -tko li - to - sci, Wi - taj, na -dzie -jo na - sza w

smu -tku i za - lo - sci.

U drzwi Twoich

U drzwi -Two -ich sto - je, Pa - nie, u drzwi Two -ich stoe -je, Pa - nie, cze -kam na Twe

zmi -lo - wa - nie, cze -kam na Twe zmi -lo - wa -nie.

Wedding March

Veni Creator Spiritus

Ve - ni Cre - á - tor Spí - ri - tus, Men - tes tu - ó - rum ví - si - ta:
Qui di - ce - ris Pa - rá - cli - tus, Al - tís - si - mi dó - num Dé - i,
Tu sep - ti - fór - mis mú - ne - re, Dígi - tus Pa - tér - næ déx - te - ræ,

Im - ple su - pér - na grá - ti - a, Quae tu cre - á - sti, pé - cto - ra.
Fons vi - vus, i - gnis, cá - ri - tas, Et spi - ri - tá - lis un - cti - o.
Tu ri - te pro - mís - sum Pa - tris, Ser - mó - ne di - tans gút - tu - ra.

A - men.

Te Deum Laudamus

Spadła Z Wiśni

Spadła z wiśni, widzieliśmy
I podarła fartuszeczek, szywaliśmy,
I podarła fartuszeczek, szywaliśmy

Jeden trzymał, drugi trzyma
A ten trzeci co doleci, porozrywał
A ten trzeci co doleci, porozrywał

Czy ci rada, czy nie rada
Musisz kochać i szanować, tego dziada,
Musisz kochać i szanować, tego dziada.

179

The Unveiling Song

As lovely green grass grows,
    throughout the promised land,
Before the main alter,
    you've given _____ your hand.
You've given _____ your hand,
    he gave a golden band,
Your eyes swelled up with tears,
    before your friends on hand.
Twelve lovely white petals
    attached to this white rose,
Twelve heavenly angels,
    serve the bride they chose.
The first angel has brought,
    a white candle's brilliance,
The second angel brought,
    a lily's full fragrance.
The third angel has brought,
    a lovely bouquet to hold,
The fourth angel has brought
    your wedding band of gold.
The fifth angel has come,
    with blessings from the Lord,
The sixth angel has come,
    with matrimonial accord.
Remaining six angels,

    come with a crown so keen,
They'll place it on your head,
    as if upon a queen.
You promised to be true,
    love, honor and obey,
In all your days ahead,
    uphold vows made today.
Remember to be good,
    and live in wedded bliss,
And in our presence now,
    honor him with a kiss.
Remember _____, be true,
    your right hand on the cross,
You've pledged your life and love,
    to _____, who is the boss.
Oh wedding gown and crown,
    somehow you make me sad,
You make me feel that I'm
    losing my mom and dad.
And yet with mom and dad,
    no longer shall you live,
But only with your _____,
    to whom your life you give.
Remember to be good,
    and live a life of prayer,
And in a year or two,
    present him with an heir.

Rośnie Trawka

1. *(repeat as needed)*

2. *(final ending)*

Rośnie Trawka

Rośnie trawka rośnie, w cieniu przy witrażu
Dałaś panu rączkę, przy wielkim Ołtarzu.
Dałaś panu rączkę, dał ci ksiądz obrączkę
Zalałaś się łzami, przed jego oczami
Dwanaście listeczków, przy tej białej róży
Dwanaście aniołów, Tobie dzisiaj służy
Pierwszy anioł niesie, świece gorejące,
Drugi anioł niesie lilije pachnące.
Trzeci anioł niesie, ten piękny wianeczek
Czwarty anioł niesie złoty pierścioneczek.
Piąty anioł niesie, od Boga małżeństwo
Szósty anioł niesie, to Błogosławieństwo.
Resztę sześć aniołów, koronę mirtową
Włoża ci na głowé, jakby na królową.
Stoją panny w rzędzie i sobie tak radzą
Wianeczek ci zdejmą a czepek ci wsadzą.
Przeżegnaj sie......, prawą rączkę na krzyż
Bo już ostatni raz, na ten wianek patrzysz.
O wianku, wianeczku, cały z róż narwany
Bardziej ci mnie go żal, niż rodzonej mamy.
Bo z mamą rodzoną nie bedé mieszkała,
Tylko z toba....., bom ci ślubowała.
żebyś była dobra, i go szanowała,
Za roczek lub za dwa, synka doczekała.

181

Money Dance

Dup-nik Traditional Wedding Dance

Appendix 3

Sources

Fashion

Amazon Drygoods
 Janet Burgess, president
 2218 East 11th Street
 Davenport, Iowa 52803-3760
 (319)322-6800
Catalog mail-order business; "purveyors of needed items for the 19th century impression." Send $7 for pattern catalog, which includes 1200 patterns for men, women, children and dolls. Send $3 for general catalog, which has everything except patterns—hats, bonnets and accessories such as lace mitts. Send $5 for shoe catalog with hundreds of styles of reproduction shoes from all periods.

Basia Dziewanowska
 41 Katherine Rd.
 Watertown, MA 02172
 (617) 926-8048
Basia is a Polish folk costume specialist who sells authentic Polish folk costumes, footwear, weavings, and folk art.

The Folk Motif
 P.O. Box 14755
 Long Beach, CA 90803
 (562)439-7380

You can order ethnic fabrics, boots, shawls, aprons and folk wear patterns. Bora and Margarita Gajicki offer a consultation service to help you get the look you want. Call or write at the above address.

Florist

Triple Oaks Nursery and Florist
Delsea Drive
Franklinville, NJ 08322
(609) 694-4274
Polish owned and operated. Lorraine can make you a traditonal bridal wreath with herbs and flowers as well as bouquets and boutonnieres for everyone in the bridal party. She will also dry your bouquets and make them into a wreath to hang in your home.

Food

Poland, Sweet Poland
Catalog of Polish Delights
135A India Street
Brooklyn, New York 11222
(718)349-2738
Offers a very wide selection of Polish gourmet specialties including mouth-watering candies, chocolates and cookies made by the best Polish confectioneries. Besides delicious candies and cookies, you will find wild mushrooms and Polish horseradish and mustard. Orders by mail only. Write or call for a pamphlet.

Miscellaneous

Carriage Association of America
RD #1 Box 115
Salem, New Jersey 08079
This should be a beginning place to write if you cannot immediately find a company that rents carriages in your area.

Hippocrene Books, Inc.
171 Madison Avenue
New York, New York 10016

(718)454-2366

Numerous books on Polish theme including dictionaries, literature, fiction, cookbooks, customs, and history.

Polish American Journal
1275 Harlem Road
Buffalo, New York 14206
1(800)422-1275

A national and international Polish American newspaper that covers politics, religion, customs, music and all news related to Poland and Polish Americans.

Polish Heritage Art Calendar
75 Warren Hill Road, Box 36 A
Cornwall Bridge, CT 06754

A beautiful art calendar with color reproductions of Poland's most famous paintings. Like any good Polish calendar it contains the names of saints for every day of the year.

Polish Peddler
1754 Boston Road
Hinckley, Ohio 44233

Carries hand-crafted items from Poland, Czechoslovakia and Russia suitable for shower favors or wedding gifts. Write for brochure.

POLAND
Primary Regions and Major Cities

Bibliography

Abramowicz, Andzej. "Sztuka Rybaków i Rzemiślników Gdańskich XI-XIII w." [Material Culture of Gdansk Fishermen and Craftsmen in the 11th-13th Centuries]; *Polska Sztuka Ludowa*. Nr.6 1954 p.323-354.

Berdecka, Anna and Turnay, Irena. *Życie Codzienne w Warzawie Okresu Oświencenia*. [Everyday Life in Warsaw during the Enlightenment];Warszawa; Państwowy Instytut Wydawniczy, 1969.

Bogucka, Maria. *Staropolskie Obyczaje w XVI-XVII Wieku.*[Old Polish Customs in the 16th and 17th Centuries]; Warszawa: Pa_stwowy Instytut Wydawniczy, 1994.

Bubak, Józef. *Księga Naszych Imion*. [The Book of Our Names] Wrocław: Zakład Narodowy Im. Ossolińskich Wydawnictwo, 1993

Bystroń, Jan Stanisław. *Dzieje Obyczajów w Dawnej Polsce Wiek XVI-XVIII. Tom II*. [History of the Customs in Old Poland in the 16th and 17th Centuries. Vol.II]; Warszawa: Państwowy Instytut Wydawniczy, 1976.

Chenczewska-Hennel. Teresa. *Rzeczpospolita w XVII Wieku w Oczach Cudoziemców*. [The Republic in the 17th Century Through the Eyes of Foreigners]; Wrocław: Zakład Narodowy Imienia Ossolińskich Wydawnictwo, 1993.

Czarnowski, Stanisław. *Biżuteria Renesansowa.*[Renaissance Jewelry]; Warszawa: Krajowa Agencja Wydawnicza. Muzeum Narodowe w Warszawie.(Pamphlet. No date)

Dekowski, Jan Piotr. "Weselne Zwyczaje Wiankowe Na Terenie Polski Środkowej."[Wedding Wreath Customs in Central Poland]; *Prace i Materiały Muzeum Archeologicznego i Etnograficznego w Łodzi. Seria Etnograficzna Nr. 18*, 1975.

Dunkling, Leslie and Gosling, William. *The Facts of File Dictionary of First Names*. London: J.M. Dent and Sons Ltd., 1983.

Federowicz, Janina and Konopińska, Joanna. *Marianna i Róża: Zycie Codzienne w Wielkopolsce w Latach 1890-1914 z Tradycji Rodzinnej.*[Marianna and Roses: Everyday Life in Greater Poland During the Years 1890-1914 Within Family Traditions]; Warszawa: Instytut Wydawniczy Pax, 1977.

Gerlich, Halina. *Narodziny, Zaślubiny, Śmierć.*[Birth, Marriage, Death]; Katowice: Śllsk Instytut Naukowy, 1984.

Gloger, Zygmunt. *Obrzęd Weselny Polski.*[Polish Wedding Customs]; Warsawa: Księgarnia Polska J. Sikorskiej, 1902.

Gloger, Z. *Encyklopedia Staropolska. Tom I-IV.* [Encyclopedia of Old Poland]; Warszawa: Wiedza Powszechna, 1985.

Gloger, Zygmunt. *Rok Polski.*[The Polish Year]; Warszawa: Jan Fiszer, 1900.

Gołęmbioski, Łukasz. *Domy i Dwory.*[Houses and Manors]; Pzemyśl: Drukiem S.F.Piltkiewicza w Pzemyślu, 1884.

Gołęmbioski, Łukasz. *Lud Polski: Jego Zwyczaje, Zabobony.*[The Polish People. Their Customs and Superstitions]; Warszawa: Drukarnia A. Gałęzowski i Społki, 1830.

Górski, Antoni. *Cnoty i Wady Narodu Szlacheckiego.*[Virtues and Failings of the Nobility]; Warszawa: Nakładem Antoniowej Górskej, 1935.

Gutkowska-Rychlewska, Maria i Taszycka, Maria. *Ubiory i Akcesoria Mody Wieku XIX.* [Fashionable Dress and Accessories in the 19th Century]; Kraków: Muzeum Narodowe w Krakowie, 1967.

Hensla, Witold and Pazdura, Jan, ed. *Historia Kultury Materialnej Polski w Zarysie. Tom VI. 1870-1918.*[History of the Material Culture in Poland in Outline. Volume VI. 1870-1918]; Wrocław: Zakład Narodowy Imienia Ossolińskich, 1979.

Kazańczuk, Mariusz. *Staropolskie Legendy Herbowe.*[Old Polish Legends of Coat-of Arms]; Wrocław: Zakład Narodowy im. Ossolińskich Wydawnictwo Polskiej Akademii Nauk, 1990.

Kopaliński, Władysław. *Opowieści O Rzeczach Powszednich.*[Stories About Everyday Things]; Warszawa; Wiedza Powszechna, 1994.

Krzywobłocka, Bożena. *Stare i Nowy Obyczaje.*[Old and New Customs]; Warszawa: Instytut Wydawniczy Zwilzków Zawowdowych, 1986.

Murczyński, Adam. *Kuchnia Staropolska.*[Old Polish Kitchen]; Warszawa: Wydawnictwa Epoka, 1990.

Nevins, Albert. *A Saint for your Name: Saints for Girls.* Huntington, Indiana: Our Sunday Visitor, Inc., 1980.

Nevins, Albert. A Saint for your Name: Saints for Boys. Huntington, Indiana: Our Sunday Visitor, Inc., 1980.

Niesiecki, Kasper. *Herbarz Polski.Tom VII.*[Polish Coat-of-Arms]; Lipsk: Nakładem i Drukiem Breitkopfa i Haertela w Lipsku 1841.

Rumel, Aleksandra. "Obrzędy Weselne We Wsi Masi." [Wedding Customs in the Village of Masi]; *Wisła*, 1901, p.7-12.

Rojek, Tadeusz. *Polski Savoir-Vivre.*[Polish Savoir-Vivre]; Warszawa: Wydawnictwo Interpress, 1984.

Rudzki, Edward. *Polskie Królowe. Tom I i II.*[Polish Queens. Volume I and II]; Warszawa: Instytut Prasy i Wydawnictw "Novum," 1990.

Smólski, G. "O Kaszubach Nadłebiańskich." [About the Kazuby at Łeba]; *Wisła*, 1901, p.321-331.

Strybel, Robert and Maria. *Polish Heritage Cookery.* Hippocrene Books, Inc. New York 1993.

Stupnicki, Hipolit. *Herbasz Polski. Tom I* [Polish Coat-of-Arms. Volume I]; Lwów. Drukiem Kornela Piffera, 1855. (Reprinted by Figaro Press, London, 1963)

Turnau, Irena. *Odzież Mieszczaństwa Warszawskiego w XVIII Wieku.*[Clothing of the Citizens of Warsaw in the 18th Century]; Wrocław: Zakład Narodowy Imienia Ossolińskich. Wydawnictwo Polskiej Akademii Nauk, 1967.

Udziela, Seweryn. *Ludowe Stroje Krakowskie i Ich Krój.* [Folk Dress of the Cracovians and Their Cut]; Kraków: Nakładem Muzeum Etnograficznego w Krakowie, 1930.

Wernichowska, Bogna. *Historie z Obrączk1 czyli Pamiętne Sluby.*[History from Wedding Rings or Memorable Marriages]; Warszawa: Wydawnictwo PTTK Kraj, 1990.

Wojcik-Góralska, Danuta. *Niedoceniana Królowa.*[The Mysterious Queen]; Warszawa: Ludowa Spóldzielna Wydawnicza, 1987.

Zielinski, G. "Zaręczyny i Zaproszenie Na Wesele." [Engagements and Invitations to Weddings]; *Wisła*, 1897, p.292-294.

Index

191

Also of Interest from Hippocrene . . .

Polish Heritage Art Calendar 1998:
A Celebration of Wilno/Vilnius
Compiled by Jacek Galazka
Introduction by Jerzy R. Krzyznowski

The town of Wilno—now Vilnius—has played a prominent role in the history of Poles, Lithuanians, Jews, Byelorussians, Tartars, Germans, and Russians. Multiethnic, open to many cultural influences from the fifteenth century, home to many writers and scholars, Wilno has always attracted painters. In this unique tribute to a remarkable town and its enchanting setting, this, the twelfth edition of the popular calendar series, is dedicated to Wilno. The fourteen reproductions in full color celebrate the beauty of the town, its churches, castles, its summers and its winters, its sons and daughters, its rivers and surrounding countryside.

24 pages • 12 x 12 • 14 color illustrations
0-7818-0551-1 • $10.95 • (640)

Other Polish Interest Titles from Hippocrene . . .

Song, Dance & Customs of Peasant Poland
Sula Benet
Preface from Margaret Mead

"This charming fable-like book is one long remembrance of rural, peasant Poland which almost does not exist anymore . . . but it is worthwhile to safeguard the memory of what one was . . . because what [Benet] writes is a piece of all of us, now in the past but very much a part of our cultural background."—*Przeglad Polski*

247 pages • illustrations
0-7818-0447-7 • $24.95hc • (209)

Polish Folk Dances & Songs: A Step-by-Step Guide
Ada Dziewanowska

The most comprehensive and definitive book on Polish dance in the English language, with in-depth descriptions of over 80 of Poland's most characteristic and interesting dances. The author provides step-by-step instruction on positions, basic steps and patterns for each dance. Includes over 400 illustrations depicting steps and movements and over 90 appropriate musical selections. Ada Dziewanowska is the artistic director and choreographer of the Syrena Polish Folk Dance Ensemble of Milwaukee, Wisconsin.

800 pages
0-7818-0420-5 • $39.50 hc • (508)

The Polish Heritage Songbook
Compiled by Marek Sart
Illustrated by Szymon Kobylinski
Annotated by Stanislaw Werner

This unique collection of 74 songs is a treasury of nostalgia, capturing echoes of a long struggle for freedom carried out by generations of Polish men and women. The annotations are in English, the songs are in Polish.

166 pages • 65 illustrations • 74 songs • 6 x 9
0-7818-0425-6 • $14.95pb • (496)

The Polish Way: A Thousand-Year History of the Poles and Their Culture
Adam Zamoyski

"Zamoyski strives to place Polish history more squarely in its European context, and he pays special attention to developments that had repercussions beyond the boundaries of the country. For example, he emphasizes the phenomenon of the Polish parliamentary state in Central Europe, its spectacular 16th century success and its equally spectacular disintegration two centuries later . . . . This is popular history at its best, neither shallow nor simplistic . . . lavish illustrations, good maps and intriguing charts and genealogical tables make this book particularly attractive."
                    —*New York Times Book Review*

422 pages • 170 illustrations • $19.95pb
0-7818-0200-8 • (176)

Cooking the Polish Way . . .

Polish Heritage Cookery, Illustrated Edition
Robert & Maria Strybel

New illustrated edition of a bestseller with 20 color photographs!
Over 2,200 recipes in 29 categories, written especially for
Americans!

"An encyclopedia of Polish Cookery and a wonderful thing to
have!"
> —*Julia Child, Good Morning America*

"Polish Heritage Cookery is the best [Polish] cookbook printed on
the English market!"
> —*Polish American Cultural Network*

915 pages • 16 pages color photographs
0-7818-0558-9 • $39.95hc • (658)

The Best of Polish Cooking, Revised Edition
Karen West

"A charming offering of Polish cuisine with lovely woodcuts
throughout."
> —*Publishers Weekly*

"Ethnic cuisine at its best."—*The Midwest Book Review*

219 pages
0-7818-0123-3 • $8.95pb • (391)

Old Warsaw Cookbook
Rysia

Includes 850 authentic Polish recipes that can be prepared in a modern American kitchen. Contains a special section on holiday foods and customs.

300 pages
0-87052-932-3 • $12.95pb • (536)

Old Polish Traditions in the Kitchen and at the Table

A cookbook and history of Polish culinary customs. Short essays cover subjects like Polish hospitality, holiday traditions, even the exalted status of the mushroom. The recipes are traditional family fare.

304 pages
0-7818-0488-4 • $11.95pb • (546)

A Treasury of Polish Aphorisms: A Bilingual Edition
Compiled and translated by Jacek Galazka

This collection comprises 225 aphorisms by eighty Polish writers, many of them well known in their native land. Sixteen pen and ink drawings by talented Polish illustrator Barbara Swidzinska complete this remarkable exploration of true Polish wit and wisdom.

140 pages • 5 1/2 x 8 1/2 • 16 illustrations
0-7818-0549-X • $14.95 • (647)

Polish Fables, Bilingual Edition
Ignacy Krasicki
Translated by Gerard T. Kapolka

Sixty-five fables by eminent Polish poet, Bishop Ignacy Krasicki, are translated into English by Gerard Kapolka. With great artistry, the author used contemporary events and human relations to show a course to guide human conduct. For over two centuries, Krasicki's fables have entertained and instructed his delighted readers. This bilingual gift edition contains twenty illustrations by Barbara Swidzinska, a well known Polish artist.

250 pages • 6 x 9
0-7818-0548-1 • $19.95hc • (646)

Glass Mountain
Twenty-Eight Ancient Polish Folktales and Fables
Retold by W.S. Kuniczak
Illustrated by Pat Bargielski

"It is an heirloom book to pass onto children and grandchildren. A timeless book, with delightful illustrations, it will make a handsome addition to any library and will be a most treasured gift."
—Polish American Cultural Network

160 pages • 6 x 9 • 8 illustrations
0-7818-0552-X • $16.95hc • (645)

Old Polish Legends
Retold by F.C. Anstruther
Wood engravings by J. Sekalski

Now, in a new gift edition, this fine collection of eleven fairy tales, with an introduction by Zygmunt Nowakowski, was first published in Scotland during World War II, when the long night of German occupation was at its darkest.

66 pages • 7 1/4 x 9 • 11 woodcut engravings
0-7818-0521-X • $11.95hc • (653)

Treasury of Polish Love Poems, Quotations & Proverbs
Miroslaw Lipinski, editor and translator

Works by Krasinski, Sienkiewicz and Mickiewicz are included among 100 selections by 44 authors.

128 pages • 0-7818-0297-0 • $11.95hc • (185)
Audiobook: 0-7818-0361-6 • $12.95 • (576)

Treasury of Classic Polish Love Short Stories in Polish and English
Edited by Miroslaw Lipinski

This charming gift volume delves into Poland's rich literary tradition to bring you classic love stories from six renowned authors, including Sienkiewicz, Irzykowski, Rittner, Nalkowska, Dygat, and Poswiatowska.These stories explore love's many romantic, joyous, as well as melancholic facets.

128 pages • 0-7818-0513-9 • $11.95hc • (603)

Pan Tadeusz
Adam Mickiewicz
Translated by Kenneth R. MacKenzie

On the 200th anniversary of Mickiewicz's birth comes a reprint of Poland's greatest epic poem in its finest English translation. For English students of Polish and for Polish students of English, this classic poem in simultaneous translation is a special joy to read. Polish and English text side by side.

553 pages • 0-7818-0033-1 • $19.95pb • (237)

The Dedalus Book of Polish Fantasy
Edited and translated by Wiesiek Powaga

Most of these stories from Polish fantastic literature appear in English for the first time.

320 pages • 5 1/2 x 8 1/4 • 1-873982-90-9 • $18.95pb • (267)

Quo Vadis
Henryk Sienkiewicz
Translated by W.S. Kuniczak
New Paperback Edition!

Written nearly a century ago and translated into over 40 languages, *Quo Vadis* has been a monumental work in the history of literature. W.S. Kuniczak, the foremost Polish American novelist and master translator of Sienkiewicz in this century, presents a modern translation of the world's greatest bestseller since 1905. An epic story of love and devotion in Nero's time, *Quo Vadis* remains without equal a sweeping saga set during the degenerate days leading to the fall of the Roman empire and the glory and agony of early Christianity.
589 pages • 6 x 9
0-7818-0550-3 • $19.95pb • (648)

In Desert and Wilderness
Henryk Sienkiewicz, edited by Miroslaw Lipinski

In traditional Sienkiewicz style, Stas and the little Nell and their mastiff Saba brave the desert and wilderness of Africa. This powerful coming-of-age tale has captivated readers young and old for a century.
278 pages • 6 x 9
0-7818 0235 0 - $19.95hc • (9)

Fire in the Steppe
Henryk Sienkiewicz, in modern translation by W.S. Kuniczak

"The *Sienkiewicz Trilogy* stands with that handful of novels which not only depict but also help to determine the soul and character of the nation they describe."—*James A. Michener*
750 pages • 6 x 9
0-7818-0025-0 • $24.95 hc • (16)

The Little Trilogy
Henryk Sienkiewicz, in a new translation by Miroslaw Lipinski

Comprised of three novellas, *The Old Servant*, *Hania*, and *Selim Mirza*, this collection will be enjoyed by the thousands of admirers of the greatest storyteller in Polish literature and the winner of the Nobel Prize for Literature in 1905.

267 pages • 6 x 9
0-7818-0293-8 • $19.95hc • (235)

Teutonic Knights, Illustrated Edition
Henryk Sienkiewicz
Translation edited by Alicia Tyszkiewicz and Miroslaw Lipinski

"Swashbuckling action, colorful characters and a touching love story . . ."   —*Publishers Weekly*

" . . . one of the most splendid achievements of Polish literature."   —*Zgoda*

" . . . a memorable, massive, breathtaking and compulsive read."—*New Horizon*

800 pages • illustrated • 6 x 9
0-7818-0433-7 • $30.00hc • (533)

All prices subject to change. **TO PURCHASE HIPPOCRENE BOOKS** contact your local bookstore, call (718) 454-2366, or write to: HIPPOCRENE BOOKS, 171 Madison Avenue, New York, NY 10016. Please enclose check or money order, adding $5.00 shipping (UPS) for the first book and $.50 for each additional book.